FINANCIAL AID FOR COLLEGE

A quick guide to everything you need to know, with the new 1996 forms!

Pat Ordovensky
Education Writer
USA TODAY

Peterson's
Princeton, New Jersey

Library of Congress Cataloging-in-Publication Data

Ordovensky, Pat.
    USA today's financial aid for college / Pat Ordovensky.
      p.   cm.
    Includes index.
    ISBN 1-56079-568-9
    1. Student aid—United States. 2. College costs—United States. 3. Parents—United States—Finance, Personal. I. USA today (Arlington, Va.) II. Title.
LB2337.4.O73 1995
378.3'0973—dc20   95-26614
                                                           CIP

Cover Illustration: Patrick Merrell

Design: CDS Design

Printed in the United States of America

10 9 8 7 6 5 4 3 2 1

Visit Peterson's Education Center on the Internet (World Wide Web) at http://www.petersons.com

TABLE OF CONTENTS

Acknowledgments

For three days every October, more than 100 admission and financial aid officers from the nation's campuses come to USA TODAY's Arlington headquarters to answer questions during the annual USA TODAY—CASE (Council for Advancement and Support of Education) College Admission and Financial Aid Hotline. Each year more than 3,000 calls are answered. Yet the computers report five times that many callers don't get through. This book is for those who didn't make it in the past and won't make it in the future.

A list of thanks must start with the experts who give their time each year to answer financial aid questions from students and parents and in the process share their expertise with this reporter. Most generous were Ron Shunk of Gettysburg College and Wendy Beckemeyer of Cottey College who, at the 1993 hotline, graciously agreed to let me visit their offices and see the financial aid process at work. I must specifically thank the ever-candid Barry McCarty of Lafayette College, a hotline regular since 1988, from whom I have learned more than anyone else about the intricacies and nuances of giving away money.

Ed Irish at William & Mary, Eleanor Morris at the University of North Carolina–Chapel Hill, Joe Russo at Notre Dame, Brenda Smith at Cottey, and Gettysburg's Ron Shunk contributed immensely by calculating financial aid packages for three hypothetical students as if they were real.

Especially helpful as I gathered information for the book were Bill Miller, director of the College Scholarship Service; Ann Buckley, a media relations person for The College Board; and Tim Christiansen of the National Association of Student Financial Aid Administrators.

At CASE, Brett Chambers, Kim Hughes, and Lisa Hatem have met the annual challenge of recruiting and scheduling hotline experts. Without them, there would be neither hotline nor book.

A debt is owed to the inspirational genius of Bob Dubill, senior editor at USA TODAY, who adeptly guided this book around the inevitable bureaucratic potholes. Also contributing at USA TODAY were Lynn Perri and her corps of graphic artists, for some of the charts and tables, and Carol Skalski, assistant extraordinaire.

At Peterson's, Carol Hupping and Bernadette Boylan ask the kinds of questions editors should ask: the kinds that keep authors' minds alert.

CHAPTER ONE

HARVARD COSTS $25,000 A YEAR

...but only 1 of 4 freshmen pay that much

You're probably a little scared, and more than a little confused—you're starting to think about college, for yourself or a member of your family. Among all the things you must consider in deciding which college is best, one question may be overriding all others: How will you pay for it?

You've probably heard stories about how expensive it is to go to college. Dozens of schools now charge more than $20,000 for one year. A few have price tags over $25,000. For four years, that's a bill in the neighborhood of $100,000.

On the lower end, the average cost at a state-operated public university is $6,200 a year. That's a four-year tab of about $25,000, still a hefty piece of change.

Adding to your confusion is the thought of applying for financial aid—the money out there to help relieve students of the financial burden of attending college.

Yes, financial aid exists. Last year $35 billion was distributed by federal and state governments and the colleges themselves. Un-counted millions came from other sources ranging from large cor-

1

AID AT THE HIGH-PRICED SCHOOLS

These are the 25 colleges charging the most for tuition, room and board in 1993–94 and the percentage of freshmen receiving financial aid:

	Cost	Pct. on Aid
Sarah Lawrence	$25,600	50%
Barnard	$25,492	60%
Yale	$25,110	46%
Tufts	$24,962	39%
Harvard & Radcliffe	$24,880	74%
Bennington	$24,850	73%
MIT	$24,800	62%
Swarthmore	$24,782	44%
Princeton	$24,650	70%
Hampshire	$24,650	52%
U. of Pennsylvania	$24,638	45%
Brown	$24,618	40%
Williams	$24,590	37%
Middlebury	$24,570	38%
Oberlin	$24,570	50%
Columbia	$24,570	50%
Tulane	$24,515	56%
Reed	$24,480	45%
Georgetown	$24,410	50%
Johns Hopkins	$24,360	50%
Chicago	$24,337	67%
Stanford	$24,310	69%
Cornell	$24,270	70%
Dartmouth	$24,249	37%
Smith	$24,236	51%

Source: The College Board

porations to philanthropists' estates to local PTAs. Most of the money received from these organizations is a gift and does not have to be repaid. The rest comes as low-interest loans to be repaid after leaving college.

You may have heard that getting the money is a long and complicated process, that it's available only to the very poor, that you're not eligible if you make more than $50,000, or that students accepting financial aid are considered second-class citizens among their peers.

In 1993 $35 billion was distributed by federal and state governments and the colleges themselves.

All of the above are common rumors about financial aid. None of them is true. But the rumors have been circulating so long that they have gained credibility as each new class of students moves through high school and begins to think about paying for college. The result is that financial aid, more than any other part of the going-to-college experience, is shrouded in myths that cause deserving students and their families to shy away from and become intimidated by the thought of asking for money.

This book is written to shatter the myths. In doing so, it will describe the many types of aid and explain the processes by which money is awarded. It will show how three hypothetical students— poor, middle-class, and affluent—get their share. And it will help you determine how much you might get.

Let's begin the myth shattering with the myths mentioned above.

MYTH I: IT'S COMPLICATED

This is the most prevalent of all. Rumors say the process of applying for aid, and deciding a student's eligibility, is so complex that an advanced math degree is required to comprehend it. The rumors are false.

The process is relatively simple. Eligibility for the overwhelming bulk of financial aid—from government and private sources—is decided by finding two numbers and subtracting one from the other. One number, the cost of attending a specific school, is easily looked up in any college directory. The other number, the amount a student and his family are expected to pay, can be calculated by anyone who knows how to figure percentages. I'll tell you how in Chapter Two.

By subtracting the expected family payment from the college's cost, a student learns the magic number that the financial aid people call Need. That's usually, but not always, the most aid a student can get. The amount he gets actually depends on a variety of factors including—more often than a student suspects—his high school report card.

But no one gets financial aid unless she asks for it. And if the process is simple, the application can be hard work. It asks a lot of questions about the student's and family's financial position that require digging out records. After you've finished, keep them out. They're records you'll need for your tax return.

At Gettysburg College in Pennsylvania, when Financial Aid Director Ron Shunk explains the process to potential applicants, he begins: "Folks, this isn't brain surgery. When you cut through it, it's a very simple process."

MYTH II: IT'S ONLY AVAILABLE TO THE POOR

False again. Some federal programs provide help only to low-income students. But others spread the wealth to anyone whose magic number—devised by the simple subtraction described on page 11—shows a financial Need. And the formula for determining how much a family should pay is devised so that even some wealthy students can wind up with a Need.

For example, at Gettysburg College where tuition, room, and board cost $24,292, two thirds of the freshmen receiving aid had family incomes over $50,000 and about 5 percent were from families with six-figure earnings. That's not unusual for a private liberal arts college in Gettysburg's price range. I'll explain how it happens in Chapter Three.

Any student can borrow money at a below-market interest rate and not start repaying until he leaves school.

After all other sources are tapped, any student can borrow money at a below-market interest rate and not start repaying until he leaves school. That's a form of financial aid.

MYTH III: FINANCIAL AID RECIPIENTS ARE SECOND-CLASS CITIZENS

Hardly. If it were true, the nation's campuses would have a very large second-class enrollment. More than half the students now attending four-year colleges are not paying the full, advertised sticker price.

Because a student's Need is directly linked to the cost of the college, the more expensive schools have more students receiving help. At Harvard, 74 percent of last year's freshmen got some kind of financial assistance. At Stanford, 67 percent received aid. At the University of Chicago, it was 68 percent.

> **More than half the students now attending four-year colleges are not paying the full, advertised sticker price.**

At Barnard College, 1995's priciest school in the country where tuition, room, and board cost $26,770 (1995 costs), 60 percent of the freshmen got some kind of financial help.

WHY THE MYSTERY?

Financial aid has developed an aura of mystery over the years because it's become a big business—a $35 billion business—with its own specialists to manage it. These specialists, who are called financial aid officers, are the only ones who fully understand a system in which others, except students, have little interest.

The administrators gather several times a year, in national and regional meetings, calling themselves "the financial aid community." They talk about need-analysis and preferential packaging, about Pells and Staffords and Perkinses, about EFC and COA and CSS and PROFILE and FAFSA.

In the old days, before 1958, the only known aid was an occasional Rotary Club scholarship, the GI Bill for military veterans, and free tuition for football players. Then, when the Soviets launched Sputnik and the U.S. was trailing badly in the space race, the government decided more scientists and engineers were needed to catch up. Encouraging college education became national public policy. In the late 1950s, Congress created a low-interest loan program to help students pay their college bills. That program, called National Defense Education Loans, eventually changed its name to what is now the government's Perkins Loans.

Lyndon Johnson's Great Society, in the late 1960s, built the framework for the current financial aid structure by creating programs of grants and subsidized jobs that offered colleges access to low-income students. Through the 1970s, Congress added new programs and tinkered with the old to make more aid available to its middle-income constituents.

The game changed dramatically in the 1980s when Ronald Reagan slashed spending in most domestic programs including college aid. The cuts came while college tuitions were climbing 6 to 12 percent a year. Colleges faced increasingly wider gaps between the prices they charged and the amount students could afford to pay.

The colleges responded by developing their own aid programs—known generically as institutional aid—in which no money changes hands but students get discounts off the published sticker price. In 1982, The College Board reported discounts totaling $1.9 billion were granted by U.S. colleges. By 1992, the total had soared to $7 billion. Students now get $1 in institutional aid for every $4 dispensed by the government.

> **Students now get $1 in institutional aid—tuition discounts from the colleges themselves— for every $4 dispensed by the government.**

And while Congress writes the rules—and changes them every few years—for federal aid programs, each school gives away its money as it sees fit. Some make it easy on themselves and their students by using the same formula as the government. Others start with the federal formula and build in variations. A few write their own rules from scratch.

> **"The more desirable a student is to an institution, the more funds the institution will use [to attract that student]."**

Adding spice to the recipe is the reality that colleges can, and do, change their rules on a case-by-case basis. If the chemistry faculty is clamoring for more students, chemistry majors could get a break on financial aid. Students who will bring up a college's SAT average could get more help than their less adept peers. A student who says that he will go to another college that offers more aid could find his tuition discount suddenly increased.

John Agett of Florida's Stetson University, who has been in the financial aid business since 1966, puts it simply: "The more desirable a student is to an institution, the more funds the institution will use [to attract that student]."

Students who understand the system gain the power to make it work for them. This book is written to empower the student.

GRANTS OR LOANS?

Almost all financial aid comes in one of two forms: a grant to a student with no strings attached or a loan. Loans are considered financial aid when they carry a below-market interest rate and need not be repaid until the student leaves college.

Grants, of course, are preferable. But just about every student who gets aid will be offered a package containing some combination of grants and loans. A loan offer doesn't have to be ac-

> **Almost all financial aid comes as an outright grant or a loan.**

cepted but the alternatives are finding the money elsewhere or finding a less-expensive school.

Financial aid administrators say in these debt-conscious times an increasing number of parents resist new loans for college expenses

> **Don't get hung up on the idea of borrowing half the cost of college. It's an investment that will pay dividends—in increased earning power.**

and opt for a less-expensive school available without borrowing. College students interviewed for this book report the same parental reluctance.

"One parent told me, I'll do anything for my kid except borrow," says Benny Walker, vice president for enrollment management at Furman University.

Students and family members reading this book for advice are about to get some. Consider carefully the advantages of a loan, if it's necessary, to pay for the college of your choice.

You probably have few reservations about borrowing 90 percent of the cost of a home. Or 75 percent of the cost of a car. Don't get hung up on the idea of borrowing half the cost of college. Given the stagnant nature of the real estate market these days, it's the only one of those three investments that will pay dividends—in increased earning power.

With all the financial aid available, cost should be one of the least-important factors in your decision about a college. Many other items in the selection process—a school's strength in specific academic areas, its size, location, the type of students it attracts—should carry greater weight in your decision.

> **Find the college that serves you best, regardless of the price; work to reduce the price. Then borrow, if you must, to get there.**

Find the college that serves you best, the school that's your best fit, regardless of the price on the windshield. Using the knowledge you've gained about financial aid from this book and elsewhere, work to reduce the sticker price as low as possible. Then borrow, if you must, to get there.

CAN COUNSELORS HELP?

Maybe. Financial aid officials and college students interviewed for this book say high school counselors' knowledge of the aid process runs the gamut from extremely high to total ignorance.

Some counselors work closely with college financial aid officers, attend their conventions, speak their language, know as much about the process as the best of them. Others barely know the difference between a Pell Grant and a Perkins Loan.

If you have one of the former, you're lucky. If not, you'll have to get personal advice from financial aid offices on the campuses you're considering. Friends who recently have gone through the process can be a big help.

HOW ABOUT OLDER STUDENTS?

Age is not a factor in the financial aid process. A 40-year-old student is subject to the same eligibility tests and finds his magic number the same way as an 18-year-old student. In some cases an older student may have an edge.

Age is not a factor in the financial aid process.

When we discuss the differences between dependent and independent students, older students by definition will be independent. Except in those cases, everything in this book applies equally to all ages.

NOW WHAT?

It's time to explain how to find your key to unlock the money vaults. After that, I'll describe what's inside after you open them. Along the way, I'll debunk a few more myths.

YOUR MAGIC NUMBER

...the key to the financial aid vaults

I t's time to start talking the way the financial aid people talk. In their jargon, your magic number is called your "Need." This Need bears little relation to the money you might actually need to attend college but it's a number you must have to start playing the game.

The higher your number the better because it's supposed to represent—in dollars—the maximum amount of aid for which you're eligible. You might get all the money you're eligible for or just a portion of it. If you're lucky and you understand the process, you could even get more than your Need.

Some colleges require you to have two magic numbers, one to trigger eligibility for government aid programs and another to use as they distribute their own money in tuition discounts. They do this because they're unhappy with the way Congress rewrote the rules for the federal programs in 1992, so they use another formula to dispense their cash. In 1995, about 500 colleges asked students to figure their Need twice.

HOW TO FIND YOUR MAGIC NUMBER

Your Need is the result of simple subtraction. You find the cost of a school to which you're applying and subtract the amount your family should pay according to the formula discussed in Chapter One. Because no two colleges' costs are identical, your magic number—or Need—will differ with each application.

The higher the cost of the college, the more financial aid you may get.

Let's say you live in Ohio and are considering Denison University and Ohio State. The cost of attending Denison in 1993 was $22,280. Ohio State was $8,724. If the formula says your family is expected to pay $3,000, your Need would be $19,280 at Denison and $5,724 at Ohio State. Thus you would be eligible for much more financial aid at Denison.

Now let's say your friend, whose family is more affluent, is applying to the same two colleges. The formula decides his family should pay $9,000. His Need at Denison would be $13,280, or $6,000 less than yours. At Ohio State—subtracting $9,000 from $8,724—it would be zero (negative numbers aren't used). Your friend would be eligible for financial aid at Denison but would get nothing from Ohio State.

These differences will be seen more dramatically when we follow three hypothetical students through the process in Chapter Seven.

Cost of Attendance – Expected Family Contribution = Need.

In financial aid jargon, the magic-number subtraction is expressed this way:

Cost of Attendance – Expected Family Contribution = Need.

FINDING YOUR COLLEGE'S COST

This is the easiest part. You can look it up. In private schools the bulk of the cost is tuition and fees. If you plan to live on campus, add room and board. Those numbers can be found in any college directory available in libraries and high school counseling offices.

COST OF ATTENDANCE

The cost of attending a college for financial aid purposes is more than just tuition, room, and board. Here is how costs would be determined for a typical college:

Tuition	$10,000
Room, board	3,950
Books, supplies	600
Transportation	350
Personal expenses	1,250
Cost of Attendance	$16,150

Your cost, for purposes of finding your magic number, also includes transportation to and from the campus, books, and personal supplies. Most colleges add a flat total—say $1,000—to tuition, room, and board to cover the other costs and to come up with the total Cost of Attendance.

Tuition + room and board (for resident students) + books + transportation + personal supplies = Cost of Attendance.

You can add $1,000 for most schools and be in the ball park. Or you can call the college financial aid office and ask the total it's using as Cost of Attendance for the current year. That's the total you use in your magic-number subtraction.

HOW COSTS ARE RISING

Here's how average cost of attendance at college has climbed in the last decade:

	4-Year Private	4-Year Public	2-Year
1983–84	$ 7,244	$3,285	$2,534
1985–86	$ 8,551	$3,637	$2,981
1987–88	$ 9,854	$4,250	$3,066
1989–90	$11,375	$4,723	$3,299
1991–92	$13,275	$5,479	$3,665
1993–94	$15,818	$6,207	$4,024

Source: The College Board

Remember: Cost of Attendance **must be** higher than tuition, room, and board for resident students and higher than tuition for commuters. If the number you get from the financial aid office is not higher, ask again.

YOUR FAMILY'S PAYMENT

If you already glanced at the worksheet accompanying this chapter, calm down. It's not as bad as it looks. You'll need the worksheet to help you determine how much you are expected to pay for a year at college—any college.

The formula is designed to weigh your financial resources against your living expenses—and your parents' resources and expenses if you are a dependent—to decide how much you can reasonably contribute to your education.

The number you get from the formula may bear little resemblance to the amount you have stashed away to pay for college. It very likely could be higher than the amount you think you can afford to pay. If so, don't despair. It's a starting point. It can be adjusted. And avenues exist, as we'll explain later, to find more money.

The formula number is called your Expected Family Contribution, usually shortened to EFC and frequently just FC. Family, in this case, can mean many things. It could be your parents' family, if you are financially dependent on them. It could be you and your spouse. If you are financially independent and living alone, your family is you. Anyone who applies for financial aid has an Expected Family Contribution.

DEPENDENT OR INDEPENDENT?

This is the first question the formula asks. The answer to this question will determine your financial status. Generally, but not always, an independent student gets a lower EFC because parents' income and assets are not taken into consideration.

In the past, the line was fuzzy. For a while, anyone who earned a certain income was considered independent regardless of where they lived. That changed in 1992 when Congress rewrote the rules. Now to be considered independent you must answer "yes" to at least one of six questions:

- Are you 24 or older?
- Are you married?
- Are you a graduate or professional student?
- Do you have dependents?
- Are you an orphan or ward of a court?
- Are you a military veteran?

Answer "yes" at least once and you're independent. Answer "no" six times and you're not.

FAFSA VS. PROFILE

Two terms essential to the vocabulary of a financial aid applicant are FAFSA and PROFILE. The reasons they're in capital letters is FAFSA is an acronym for a government form and PROFILE is the name given to a form by the company that produces it.

Parents and older siblings may fondly remember the FAF, which stands simply for Financial Aid Form. For years, it was the most common form used to apply for money. By 1995, as PROFILE made its debut, FAF was relegated to the dust bin of forms that outlive their usefulness.

FAFSA is the form everyone now files to determine his or her Expected Family Contribution.

The FAFSA, officially the Free Application for Federal Student Aid, now is the form everyone files. The information it contains is plugged into the formula that determines Expected Family Contribution, and thus your magic number, for most government aid programs.

Many colleges keep it simple by using the same Need number for their own programs. But about 500 schools want you to have two numbers—one for the government and one for them. That means you must submit two forms, the FAFSA and the PROFILE. The PROFILE duplicates much

> **About 750 schools want you to submit both the FAFSA and the PROFILE.**

of the information on the FAFSA and asks for additional stuff—such as the value of your parents' home—that some colleges like to know. Both forms are required by almost all high-priced private colleges, including the eight Ivy League schools.

Some colleges will ask you to submit a PROFILE in the fall of your senior year so they can get an early estimate of your Need. Others want it the same time you file the FAFSA, after January 1. If a college wants a PROFILE, it will let you know.

For purposes of figuring your magic number, we print both forms in Chapter Four and include a worksheet for the FAFSA.

THE GOVERNMENT FORMULA

Much of the information needed by the government comes from the student's and parents' tax returns. If you haven't done your taxes before you apply for financial aid, estimates are acceptable.

You'll see how it works as you figure your EFC from the worksheet on page 16 and 17. If you have your records handy, completing the worksheet should take five to ten minutes.

In Part I of the worksheet, just enter parents' income as it will be reported to the IRS.

In Part II, list expenses to be deducted from parents' income. They include federal income tax and other taxes computed in Tables 1–4, and an Income Protection Allowance that's supposed to cover the cost of basic living expenses. As you see from Table 4, it varies by family size. Financial aid officers admit the allowance is very low, barely above poverty level.

In Part III, simple subtraction produces the parents' income to be used in the formula.

WORKSHEET FOR
CALCULATING YOUR CONTRIBUTION
THE GOVERNMENT'S WAY

(Income and taxes are from tax returns for the year before the application is filed. For example, applicants in winter/spring 1996 use 1995 figures. If firm numbers are unavailable, estimates are permitted.)

Parents' Contribution
- I.   Income
  Parents' adjusted gross income $ _____
  Untaxed income including IRA contribution   + _____
  Total Income   _____ (A)
- II.   Allowances
  Federal income tax $ _____
  State and other taxes (Table 1)   + _____
  Social Security taxes (Table 2)   + _____
  Employment allowance (Table 3)   + _____
  Income protected (Table 4)   + _____
  Total Allowances   _____ (B)
- III.   Available Income (Line A – Line B) $ _____ (C)
- IV.   Assets
  Cash in bank accounts $ _____
  Investment equity (excluding residence)   + _____
  Business adjusted net worth (Table 5)   + _____
  Net Worth   _____
  Asset Protection Allowance (Table 6)   – _____
  Discretionary Net Worth (DNW)   _____ (D)
- V.   Available Assets (12% of DNW) $ _____
- VI.   Adjusted Available Income* (Line C + Line D) $ _____
- VII.   Parents' Total Contribution (Table 7) $ _____

- A.   Contribution to Student $ _____ (E)
  (Parents' contribution divided by number of family members in college.)

Student's Contribution
- I.   Income
  Student's adjusted gross income $ _____
  Untaxed income   + _____
  Total Income   _____ (F)

* Parents adjusted available income can be a negative number.

II. Allowances
    Federal income tax $ _____
    State and other taxes (Table 1)   + _____
    Social Security taxes (Table 2)   + _____
    Income protected   + \$1,750
    Total Allowances   _____(G)
III. Available income (Line F – Line G) $ _____(H)
IV. Contribution from income (50% of Line H) $ _____ (I)
 V. Assets (cash in banks, investment equity) $ _____(J)
VI. Contribution from assets (35% of Line I) $ _____(K)

B. Student's Contribution (Line I + Line K) $ _____ (L)

C. Expected Family Contribution (Line E + Line L) $ _____

In Part IV, list parents' assets such as stocks, bonds, and savings accounts. Use Table 6 to determine how much of those assets are protected, or exempt from the formula. (This is where older parents get a break because the exempt amount increases with age. Financial aid people feel that as parents move closer to retirement they should spend less of their nest egg on college.) Then, with your calculator, figure 12 percent of the assets that are left unprotected.

In Part V, add the parents' available income and assets, then use that number to calculate from Table 7 the amount the student's parents are expected to pay for a year at college. Divide that by the number of family members in college (who are taking at least six credits) and you have the parental contribution for each student.

Then you go through a similar process for the student— information on income, expenses, and assets will be needed. If a student earned less than \$1,750 last year and has no assets, she'll be expected to pay nothing.

Add the parents' and student's contributions and you have your Expected Family Contribution.

Remember the subtraction formula at the start of this chapter:

Cost of Attendance – Expected Family Contribution = Need.

Presto! There's your magic number.

TABLE 1
STATE AND OTHER TAXES

Apply the percentage below to Total Income on the worksheet

Parents

10%	New York
9%	District of Columbia, Oregon, Wisconsin
8%	Maine, Maryland, Massachusetts, Michigan, Minnesota, Rhode Island
7%	California, Delaware, Hawaii, Iowa, Montana, Nebraska, New Jersey, North Carolina, Ohio, South Carolina, Utah, Vermont, Virginia
6%	Colorado, Georgia, Idaho, Kansas, Kentucky, New Hampshire, Pennsylvania
5%	Arizona, Arkansas, Connecticut, Illinois, Indiana, Missouri, New Mexico, North Dakota, Oklahoma, West Virginia
4%	Alabama, Mississippi
3%	Florida, Louisiana, South Dakota, Washington, Puerto Rico, Virgin Islands
2%	Alaska, Nevada, Tennessee, Texas, Wyoming

Students

7%	District of Columbia, New York
6%	Hawaii, Maryland, Minnesota
5%	California, Delaware, Idaho, Iowa, Kentucky, Maine, Massachusetts, Montana, North Carolina, Ohio, South Carolina, Utah, Wisconsin
4%	Arkansas, Colorado, Georgia, Indiana, Kansas, Michigan, Nebraska, New Mexico, Rhode Island, Vermont, Virginia, West Virginia
3%	Alabama, Arizona, Mississippi, Missouri, New Jersey, Pennsylvania
2%	Connecticut, Illinois, Louisiana, North Dakota, Puerto Rico, Virgin Islands
1%	Florida, New Hampshire
Zero	Alaska, Nevada, South Dakota, Tennessee, Texas, Washington, Wyoming

IF YOU'RE INDEPENDENT

It's even easier if you answered "yes" to one of the six questions above and the formula considers you financially independent. You

TABLE 2
SOCIAL SECURITY TAXES

Earned Income
  $57,600 or less: 7.65% of income earned by each person; maximum
                     $4,406 per person
  Over $57,600: $4,406 plus 1.45% of income over $57,600;
                     maximum $5,529 per person

can skip the Parents' Contribution. Just enter information for you and your spouse (if you have one) in the students' section. An instant EFC!

THE MARRIAGE PENALTY

An unmarried couple need not report each other's income. A married couple reports both spouses' incomes. If your girlfriend earns $50,000 a year, that money is ignored as the formula calculates how much you should pay for college. If you get married, her income will become a factor in determining how much you should pay for college.

That's not the only marriage penalty Congress has written into the law. If a student's natural parents are divorced and the custodial parent is re-married, the government formula considers incomes of the parent and step-

Spouses incomes must be reported.

parent. So a student living with a divorced mother loses some of her financial aid—at least her Need is lower—if Mom gets remarried.

TABLE 3
EMPLOYMENT ALLOWANCE

Two parents: 35% of lower earned income; maximum $2,500
One parent: 35% of earned income; maximum $2,500

TABLE 4
INCOME PROTECTION ALLOWANCE

Family Size*	Family Members in College				
	1	2	3	4	5
2	10,840	8,980			
3	13,490	11,650	9,800		
4	16,670	14,810	12,970	11,110	
5	19,660	17,810	15,970	14,110	12,270
6	23,000	21,250	19,300	17,450	15,600

* For each additional family member in college, add $2,600.

THE COLLEGES' FORMULA

You may have noticed, as you went through the government worksheet, that when you listed parents' stocks, bonds, and savings accounts you did not include their home. Equity in a home is not considered an asset when the government computes your Need. Until 1993, it was.

Home equity sparked the hottest debate between Congress and financial aid officials as the rules were revised. Congress decided it's unfair to penalize parents whose home values soared in the 1980s. Financial aid officials argued it's unfair not to include home equity as an asset.

> **Equity in a home is no longer considered an asset on FAFSA, but it is on PROFILE.**

TABLE 5
BUSINESS ADJUSTED NET WORTH

Net Worth	Adjusted Net Worth
Less than $1	0
$1 to $75,000	40% of Net Worth
$75,001 to $250,000	$30,000 + 50% of Net Worth over $75,000
$230,001 to $385,000	$107,500 + 60% of Net Worth over $230,000
Over $385,000	$200,500 + 100% of Net Worth over $385,000

TABLE 6
ASSET PROTECTION ALLOWANCE

Age of Older Parent	Married	Single
25 or younger	0	0
26	2,100	1,500
27	4,300	3,100
28	6,400	4,600
29	8,600	6,200
30	10,700	7,700
31	12,900	9,200
32	16,000	10,800
33	17,200	12,300
34	19,300	13,900
35	21,500	15,400
36	23,600	16,900
37	25,800	18,500
38	27,900	20,000
39	30,100	21,600
40	32,200	23,100
41	33,000	23,500
42	33,900	24,100
43	34,700	24,500
44	35,400	25,100
45	36,300	25,600
46	37,200	26,200
47	38,500	26,900
48	39,400	27,500
49	40,500	28,000
50	41,500	28,700
51	42,800	29,400
52	43,900	30,300
53	45,300	31,000
54	46,700	31,800
55	47,900	32,500
56	49,400	33,500
57	50,900	34,300
58	52,500	35,300
59	54,400	36,300
60	56,000	37,200
61	58,100	38,200
62	59,800	39,300
63	61,900	40,400
64	64,100	41,800
65 or older	66,300	42,900

TABLE 7
PARENTS' CONTRIBUTION

Adjusted Available Income (AAI) from worksheet*	Parents' Contribution
– $3,408 or less	– $750
– $3,409 to + $9,700	22% of AAI
$9,701 to $12,200	$2,134 + 25% of AAI over $9,700
$12,201 to $14,600	$2,759 + 29% of AAI over $12,200
$14,601 to $17,100	$3,455 + 34% of AAI over $14,600
$17,101 to $19,600	$4,305 + 40% of AAI over $17,100
$19,601 or more	$5,305 + 47% of AAI over $19,600

* Can be a negative number.

William Miller, who heads the formula-processing service for The College Board, says many colleges "believe fairly strongly that, any way you slice it, a family that has home equity has an element of financial strength that simply is not there for a family that is renting."

When Congress dropped home equity from the government formula, hundreds of colleges decided they still would consider it as they give away their own money. Thus many students must submit two forms—one from the government and one from the college—and get two magic numbers.

In the college formula, the procedure and much of the information requested is the same as for the government. The big difference is home equity must be listed as an asset for parents and independent students.

Some other differences:

- In the government formula, a student's expected contribution can drop to zero. The colleges' formula lets it go no lower than $900. The colleges, says Miller, have "some minimum expectations from the students personally before they go looking for additional resources."

- The colleges' formula includes medical and dental expenses (if they are at least 4% of income) and tuition paid to private elementary and secondary schools as deductible expenses from income. The government doesn't.

> **On FAFSA a student's expected contribution can drop to zero, but on PROFILE the least it can be is $900.**

The additions, subtractions, and percentage calculations are the same in both formulas.

Now that you have worked through both forms you have two EFCs. And two magic numbers.

The worksheet is printed on pages 16 and 17 so you can get an idea of how you'll fare in the financial aid quest and how high your all-important Need is likely to be. When you apply, your real magic number will be determined by a computer you've never met. But if the numbers you used on the worksheet are the same as those you enter on your application, you and the computer will be very close.

> **PROFILE deducts medical and dental expenses (if they are at least 4% of income) and private school tuition; FAFSA doesn't.**

It's time to see what your magic number can do. How your Need will be filled.

CHAPTER THREE

THE MANY KINDS OF AID

...grants, loans, and other types of money for college

Financial aid can be a gift that you keep or a loan that you must repay. It can come from the government, from your college, or from some other source. It can be paid directly to the student, to the student's school, or to the student's parents.

Each financial aid program was conceived and grew up independently of all others, designed to serve a specific need. The only place they come together is in the financial aid office on each college campus. That's where the student learns how much he will get, from whom, and in what form.

The process of putting it together is called packaging. The college financial aid director prepares each student's aid package, playing by the rules written by the people who provide the money. And some rules, as we'll see in Chapter Six, give the financial aid director considerable flexibility.

The largest benefactor in the financial aid business is, was, and probably always will be the federal government. Its slice of the financial aid pie shrunk during the cuts of the Reagan years but still

$3 of every $4 spent to help students through college comes from Washington.

The government has four major aid programs—two offering grants, two making loans—and some smaller efforts targeted at specific audiences. It also spends about $760 million a year subsidizing students' campus jobs, another form of aid.

As federal spending declined, colleges increased the amount of aid that they offered—most in the form of tuition discounts. And most, but not all, is based on a student's Need. Other players are state governments, corporations, foundations, service clubs, fraternities and sororities, and scores of other organizations.

Let's look at how the programs work.

PELL GRANTS

The first and by far the largest source of grants is named for Sen. Claiborne Pell, D-R.I. Last year, 3.7 million students shared more than $6.5 billion in Pell Grants.

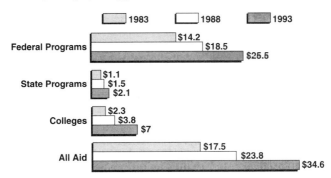

WHERE AID COMES FROM

Most aid still comes from Washington but, over the last 10 years, colleges have been picking up a bigger share from their own funds (in billions):

☐ 1983   ☐ 1988   ▨ 1993

Federal Programs
$14.2
$18.5
$25.5

State Programs
$1.1
$1.5
$2.1

Colleges
$2.3
$3.8
$7

All Aid
$17.5
$23.8
$34.6

Source: The College Board

The largest source of grants are Pell Grants, designed to help low-income students pay for college.

The Pell program was created 25 years ago—then they were called Basic Opportunity Grants—to provide college access for low-income students. Pell Grants often are described as the "foundation" on which financial aid packages are built.

Eligibility for a Pell is determined solely by a student's Estimated Family Contribution generated by the government's formula. Last year, any student with an EFC under $2,100 was eligible. That could change for the 1995–96 school year.

When you apply for financial aid, you automatically apply for a Pell Grant. When the government's computers inform you of your EFC, they tell you if it's low enough to qualify for a Pell.

If you're eligible you'll get a grant ranging from the $400 minimum up to the maximum, which is set each year by the amount of money Congress appropriates to the program. Last year the maximum grant was $2,300. The size of your grant is determined by a scale linked directly to that magic number—your Need. The average grant in 1994 was $1,518.

A Pell Grant is paid to the college which then credits the student's account. Don't be fooled by headlines you might read saying Congress has increased the Pell to $4,500 or another higher number. In recent years Congress has authorized higher Pell Grants but, when the time came to put money in the pot, declined to fund them at the higher level.

In 1994 the average Pell Grant was $1,518; the maximum was $2,300.

SUPPLEMENTAL EDUCATIONAL OPPORTUNITY GRANTS

The other large federal grant program usually appears in college literature as SEOGs. In conversation, the grants often are called "supplementals" or, by veteran financial aid officers, "sogs" (because they were SOGs before someone inserted Educational into their title).

SEOGs, as the name implies, are used to enhance educational opportunities for low-income students provided by Pell Grants. They're also available to students with a high Need. Last year, $583 million in SEOGs went to about 1 million students.

Unlike the Pell, which any eligible student receives directly from the government, SEOGs are in a category called campus-based aid. That means each school's financial aid office gets an annual lump sum to distribute under certain rules, as it desires.

Many colleges give SEOGs only to their Pell Grant recipients with the lowest EFCs. Some save a little for students who don't qualify for a Pell but still have a high Need. The maximum SEOG is $4,000 but, to spread the money among more students, most schools make grants in the $500–$1,000 range. The average in 1994 was $583.

> **SEOGs are government grants distributed by colleges to its most needy students. Last year the average SEOG was $583; the maximum was $4,000.**

WORK-STUDY

Anyone who has attended college in the last 20 years knows this program as College Work-Study or CWS. Since last year it has been Federal Work-Study or FWS. But only the name has changed. It's still a form of working your way through college with government help.

Walk into any office on any campus and the student you see filing papers or answering phones is probably earning Work-Study money.

Like SEOGs, Work-Study is a campus-based program. Each school gets an annual lump sum from the government to pay 75 percent of a student's wages at campus or community jobs. The jobs are lined

Federal Work-Study subsidizes campus jobs for students who have a Need. In 1994, the average annual Work-Study wage was $1,066.

up by the college financial aid office and assigned as part of a student's aid package. Each job must pay an hourly wage—no commissions or fees—of at least $4.25.

Any student with a Need—an EFC lower than the Cost of Attendance—is eligible for Work-Study. Qualifying for a Pell Grant isn't necessary. But the higher your Need, the more likely the financial aid folks will offer you a job.

Work-Study wages are paid to the student to use for whatever expenses she chooses. In 1994, about 713,000 students had Work-Study jobs subsidized by $583 million of federal money. The average annual wage for Work-Study jobs was $1,066.

PERKINS LOANS

This program started it all in 1958, when the government offered low-interest loans to encourage kids to go to college. It has been renamed for the late Rep. Carl Perkins, D-Ky., long-time chair of the House Education and Labor Committee.

Perkins is the only loan program that's campus based. Colleges get a lump sum, which they loan to students who have Need. As the loans are repaid, the money is circulated into new loans. Some colleges don't participate because of the time, effort, and paperwork required to process the loans.

An undergraduate can borrow $3,000 a year up to a maximum of $15,000. A graduate student can get $5,000 a year but his total Perkins debt cannot surpass $30,000.

The advantage of a Perkins is the lowest interest rate—around 5 percent. Repayment need not begin until nine months after a student leaves college. A student can take up to 10 years to repay the loan, but the college can require minimum monthly payments of $40. (To circulate the money faster, some colleges sell Perkins Loans to banks, which then become the collection agencies.)

The government's regulations say Perkins Loans should go to students with exceptional Need, then they allow each financial aid office to define "exceptional" according to its own guidelines. As a rule, the higher your magic number, the more likely a Perkins Loan will be offered as part of your aid package.

Perkins Loans are government-funded low-interest loans distributed by colleges. An undergraduate can borrow up to $3,000 a year, for a maximum of $15,000.

In 1994, 697,000 students got Perkins Loans worth a total of $600 million. The average loan was $1,334.

SUBSIDIZED LOANS

Parents may fondly remember the Guaranteed Student Loans, or GSLs, which helped millions of their generation get a degree. Here they are, dressed in new clothes with new names.

A subsidized loan typically is the cap on a student's financial aid package. The aid office pulls together as much as it can in grants, Work-Study, and Perkins Loans. If the total is less than your Need, you get the opportunity to apply for a subsidized loan. It's your magic number working for you.

Subsidized loans now come by two names: Direct Loans and FFELs (Federal Family Education Loans). Don't worry about the difference because it's important only to colleges, the government, and bankers. The names merely identify the source of the money you borrow. The college will decide which you get.

FFELs also are called FFEL Stafford Loans. The whole loan program once was known as Stafford but now—to add to your confusion—both names are being used. Don't let them confuse you. If one college talks about FFELs and another talks about Stafford loans, they are talking about the same thing. In the charts and tables of this book, they're called Stafford loans because that's the term to which most folks are accustomed.

They're called subsidized loans because the government pays the interest, a subsidy, while the student is in college. A student can borrow up to $2,625 as a freshman, $3,500 as a sophomore, $5,500 a year as a junior or senior. A graduate student can borrow $8,500 a year but his total subsidized debt—graduate and undergraduate—can't top $65,000. The interest rate is adjusted every June but can go no higher than 8.25 percent. For loans obtained in the year ending June 30, 1995, the rate was 7.43 percent.

Like Perkins Loans, no credit record or collateral is needed to qualify for a subsidized loan. The only requirement is to be enrolled in a college and have a Need.

Low-interest subsidized loans are available to all students with a Need through a bank or other lending institution.

If you are offered a Direct Loan, you'll get the money directly from the college which got it from the government. If you are offered an FFEL (or Stafford) you must apply for it at a bank and the college must certify that you qualify. A standard application form is available at college financial aid offices.

Repayment must begin six months after a student leaves college but the terms are highly flexible. The rules say a student has up to 10 years to repay the loan but allows the lending institution to grant a longer period on request.

The student also has the option of making flexible monthly payments on an "income-sensitive" schedule. That means your monthly payment is based on your financial condition. The lending institution is required by law to offer you this option six months before your first payment is due.

UNSUBSIDIZED STUDENT LOANS

In Chapter One, I said anyone can get financial aid. This is it. Even you wealthy folks with zero Need can be eligible.

The unsubsidized student is the new kid on the block, born in the 1993–94 school year. It was conceived by Congress in response to complaints from middle-income constituents that they were being priced out of a college education.

In principle, it works the same as its subsidized sibling. Interest rates are the same and all the flexible repayment options apply. Like its sibling, it can come as a Direct Loan from the college or an FFEL from a bank.

The loans are called unsubsidized because there is no subsidy— the interest that accrues while the student is in college must be paid by the student. He can pay it monthly or let it ride until he leaves school, when it will be added to the principal.

Any student who thinks her aid from other sources isn't enough can apply for an unsubsidized student loan.

Any college student who thinks, from her own vantage point, that her financial aid from other sources isn't enough, can apply for an unsubsidized loan on the same standard form used for the subsidized loans—no Need is required.

If you are a dependent student, maximum loans are the same in both programs. If you're independent—if you answered "yes" to any of the six questions in Chapter Two—the unsubsidized maximums go up to $6,625 for freshmen, $7,500 for sophomores, $10,500 for juniors and seniors.

Let's look at some examples:

1. You are 18, a high school senior, applying to Old Siwash U. Your Estimated Family Contribution, determined by the government formula, is $4,000. At Old Siwash, the Cost of Attendance is $13,400. Your Need—your magic number—is $9,400.

The financial aid office at Old Siwash gives you a $500 SEOG, a $1,500 Work-Study job, and $6,000 of OSU's own money. That totals $8,000. It offers you a $1,400 subsidized student loan to cover the rest of your Need.

You think that's not enough. There's no way you and your family can come up with $4,000 as the formula says you should. Maybe $3,000, but not $4,000.

You'll be a freshman so you can apply for an unsubsidized student loan of $1,225, which is the $2,625 maximum minus the $1,400 subsidized student loan you were already offered.

So, all together you will borrow $2,625 for one year of a college education. As we noted earlier, you probably borrowed more for your car, which pays no dividend.

2. You're the student in Example 1 but you decide to forget college after high school and join the Army. Three years later, at age 21, you're a civilian and apply to Old Siwash.

As a military veteran, you're now officially independent. Although you're living at home, your parents' income and assets aren't counted in figuring your Estimated Family Contribution, which the formula computes as $500.

Your Need at OSU is $12,900. With your low EFC, you get a $1,400 Pell Grant, a $1,000 SEOG, a $1,500 Work-Study job, and a $3,000 Perkins Loan. OSU gives you $6,000 of its own cash.

Your entire $12,900 Need is covered. You still can borrow $500 in an unsubsidized student loan to meet the entire $13,400 Cost of Attendance.

3. You're the best friend of the student in Example 1, also applying to Old Siwash, but your family is better off financially. The formula says your parents should contribute $15,500 to your college expenses.

Whoa! That's more than Old Siwash costs. Your Need is zero.

You also have applied to Princeton where the Cost of Attendance —including books, transportation, and other expenses—is $27,165. Your Need at Princeton is $11,665.

Parents can take out a low-interest Plus Loan to pay for college costs not covered by a financial aid package.

At Old Siwash, you have no magic number to trigger the aid programs. But you still can borrow $2,625 in an unsubsidized student loan, payable after you leave school.

At Princeton, your magic number—$11,665—is high. Because you're an excellent student and a good musician, and because you have a Need, Princeton assembles a financial aid package of grants, Work-Study, and Perkins Loans to cover the entire $11,665. And you still can borrow $2,625 unsubsidized.

Your out-of-pocket cost to attend Princeton is just $2,000 more than at Old Siwash despite the $14,000 difference in their price tags.

PLUS LOANS

PLUS stands for Parent Loans for Undergraduate Students and that's what they are. A parent may borrow at low interest any sum between a student's Cost of Attendance and his other financial aid. Need is not considered.

If Old Siwash gives you an aid package worth $3,400 and its cost is $13,400, your parents can borrow up to $10,000 in a PLUS Loan. The money can be used only for college expenses. The check is sent to the school, co-payable to the parent borrower.

The PLUS interest rate is adjusted each June. For the year beginning July 1, 1994, it was 8.38 percent. The loan application is made to a bank with the college certifying the eligible amount. Repayment starts immediately.

INSTITUTIONAL AID

We mentioned it in the examples above. Old Siwash gave you $6,000 of its own money. Princeton offered an attractive package because you're a good student.

Institutional aid is the generic term covering all financial help offered by a college from its own resources. In 1994, the College Board reports, institutional aid topped $8 billion nationally. Most of it comes with discounts off the published sticker price.

A college giving away its money makes its own rules. Thus, institutional aid is the portion of the package that is most flexible, most open to negotiation. (I'll discuss negotiating tactics in Chapter Six.)

Institutional aid is the money colleges themselves give away. It's more prevalent at high-priced schools.

Institutional aid is most prevalent at private colleges where the tuition is high. To stay competitive in a student-buyer's market, they must help students meet their cost. It's virtually nonexistent at smaller state colleges where tuition is low, and state law often prohibits discounts.

When institutional aid exists, the line starts to blur between need-based and merit-based financial aid. All other aid programs fall neatly into one of those two categories. The large government programs are based solely on a student's need, but some smaller grants are awarded for academic talent. The National Merit Scholarships and many grants from private organizations are for academics or talent, not need. For institutional aid, need and merit begin to blend. A college wants to use its funds to help needy students, but it prefers talented needy students.

Many financial aid directors insist their institutional aid is awarded strictly on Need. They probably mean it. No magic number, no tuition discount.

Others say they must respond to campus political pressures and consider merit more than need. David Erdmann, dean of admissions and student financial planning at Florida's Rollins College, told colleagues at a 1994 convention that he ignores many needy but less-talented applicants and uses tuition discounts to lure high-ability students. Erdmann says he must satisfy the clamor from Rollins' faculty for students with high SAT scores. Some of his cynical brethren call it "buying students."

The more talented the applicant, often the more generous the aid package.

Then there are financial aid offices that try to serve both masters. As Ron Shunk at Gettysburg College deftly puts it, he awards some money "on need-based merit."

And some blend both goals nicely. Many colleges have separate scholarship programs listed in their catalogs that award grants for academic merit and for special talent in fields such as music, theater, science, math, and athletics. They use their financial aid offices only to meet Need.

How do you know the policy of the school you're considering? You don't. All you can do is ask and observe. Some financial aid offices will answer candidly, some won't. If you are offered a package that includes institutional aid, ask specific questions about how the amount was determined. The answers could give you clues on negotiating for more.

If a school offers institutional aid, it's limited by a budget. Erdmann says he's allowed to use discounts to decrease Rollins College tuition income by 27 percent. Others in the business say their caps

The first people in line have the best shot at the money.

are around 12 to 15 percent. Gettysburg's Shunk says he can spend $11.2 million in discounts. When it's gone, it's gone. That's why all literature on the financial aid process urges students to apply early.

Shunk says he meets the formula-defined Need of all students but he's not sure how much longer that can happen.

But when Shunk and others like him meet a student's Need, it's not the same Need that the government meets with Pell Grants. Remember the PROFILE and FAFSA? If you apply to Gettysburg, you must submit both financial aid forms. You get two magic numbers, one triggering eligibility for government programs, the other for Shunk's $11.2 million pot. If the FAFSA formula says your Gettysburg Need is $11,000 and PROFILE says it's $8,000, Shunk guarantees he'll meet the lower number.

And like most of Shunk's colleagues at private colleges, the main reason he goes with the PROFILE is that it considers home equity.

"Families that own a home are in better financial condition," he says. "We're going to make our decisions for institutional funds on the fact that they've got some financial strength there."

At Pennsylvania's Lafayette College, Financial Aid Director Barry McCarty says: "The parental contribution is based on ability to pay, not a willingness to pay. Colleges assume that educating your child is a top financial priority."

GOVERNMENT MERIT AID

Although Congress pours most of its financial aid into need-based programs, it doesn't ignore academic talent. These are the government's larger merit-based awards:

- **Byrd Scholarships:** Grants of $1,500 a year to outstanding high school graduates, renewable annually for four years. Each state's scholarship agency selects winners in its state. (To obtain a listing of state scholarship agencies, contact the State Department of Education in your state.)
- **Paul Douglas Teacher Scholarships:** Grants of $5,000 a year (but not higher than the student's Cost of Attendance) to outstanding high school graduates who plan to teach in elementary or secondary schools. They're renewable

annually for four years. A student must agree to teach two
years for each year he gets the money. Winners selected by
state scholarship agencies.

- **National Science Scholars:** Grants to encourage outstanding
  high school seniors to study science, math, or engineering.
  Maximum grant is $5,000, renewable for four years, but
  actual grant varies by amount Congress appropriates each
  year. Last year, it was $2,750. Winners are selected by state
  agencies.

PRIVATE SCHOLARSHIPS

Much of the private scholarship money is restricted. It could be
ticketed for students of a certain religious faith or ethnic heritage, to
children of military veterans or union members, to Eagle Scouts or
soccer players or journalism majors or females who want to be
architects.

The money won't come to you. You have to look for it. Dozens
of directories attempt to list most of the private scholarships and
their eligibility requirements. Chances are good such a book is in
your local library, if not your high school guidance office. An easier
search tool is one of several commercial computer programs, mar-
keted to high schools and libraries, that allows you to enter a personal profile and then churns out a list of the scholarships for which
you could qualify.

But be aware that private scholarships can change the amount of
financial aid you get from a college. Some schools automatically reduce the financial package by the amount of outside scholarships. Others ignore any outside money. Still others consider it case-by-case.

SPECIALLY TARGETED AID

Congress has created several financial aid programs designed to
help specific groups. Among them:

- **Nursing Students:** Loans at 5 percent interest for nursing students with a financial need. Up to $2,500 may be borrowed the first year, $4,000 a year thereafter. Financial aid offices at schools with nursing programs select the recipients.
- **Veterans:** The current GI Bill offers education benefits of up to $350 a month for three years to veterans who have three years active duty or two years active duty and four years in the reserves.
- **Veterans' Dependents:** Dependents of veterans killed or permanently disabled by a service-related injury can get $404 a month for education expenses until age 26. The program is administered by the U.S. Department of Veterans Affairs.
- **Native Americans:** The U.S. Bureau of Indian Affairs administers the program of need-based grants to students who are more than 25 percent Indian, Eskimo, or Aleut. Information can be obtained from BIA offices.
- **Pharmacists:** The Health Education Assistance Loan program, targeted chiefly at graduate and professional students, offers low-interest loans to undergraduates studying pharmacy. Recipients are selected by financial aid offices.

That's what's available. Now let's look at how you get it.

HOW TO GET
THE MONEY

...time and effort can bring welcome rewards

It's not supposed to be fun. There are many things you would rather do on a winter evening than print numbers neatly in little boxes. But it's the necessary first step toward obtaining the money that's waiting out there to help you pay your college bills.

Filling out the forms to apply for aid is not a difficult task. The instructions for the most part are straightforward and written in easy-to-understand language.

But it can be tedious, time-consuming, and traumatic. It will take two to three hours to do it right. It will be tedious because detail is required and accuracy is essential. It will be traumatic because it will require students and parents to bare their financial souls.

Despite the unpleasantness of the task, all students applying to college—any college—owe it to themselves to fill out the forms. Consider it an investment of two to three hours of your time for rewards you may not have expected. Financial aid of which you're unaware may be available to you. But you won't know unless you ask.

Prepare yourself for the trauma of financial disclosure. You may not like it, but it's necessary. If you borrow money to buy a home or car, your bank will ask for the same information, which you'll provide willingly because you want the home or the car. Is college a less important investment?

At times, financial aid directors encounter parents who withdraw their children's college applications rather than disclose their personal financial situation on an aid request form. A student interviewed for this book says she is attending a college where she can pay her own way, and will transfer to another one later, because her father refuses to provide information for the financial aid forms. These parents are preserving their privacy at the expense of their children's education.

HOW MANY FORMS?

You may have to fill out just one form, probably no more than two, depending on the colleges to which you're applying.

All schools use the Free Application for Federal Student Aid (FAFSA). As mentioned earlier, about 500 colleges also require the PROFILE produced by The College Board or a similar form from another company. A few colleges—and the number is decreasing—have their own in-house supplemental forms. And some may even ask certain students to fill out yet another form. If, for example, your parents are divorced, a college might want a disclosure form from your noncustodial parent.

The good news is you'll fill out each form only once, even if you're applying to more than one college.

You'll fill out one or probably no more than two different forms, each only once, even if you're applying to six schools.

On the FAFSA, you can list six colleges to whom you want your financial information sent. And you can have it sent to even more after your data has been processed. There is no cost for this service, that's why the word "Free" is in the form's title.

The PROFILE lets you identify ten colleges to receive the information. It charges $14.50 per college and another $5.50 if you want to get a copy of the information it sends out.

WHERE ARE THE FORMS?

Most high school guidance offices have copies of the FAFSA and many also have the forms on which you apply for a PROFILE. If yours doesn't you can write to the college financial aid office and request an application package. Do it at the same time you write for an admission application.

If you are considering six colleges, **Get financial aid forms** write to all six for financial aid appli- **from all schools you're** cations. You still complete the basic **interested in.** forms only once, but if one of the six schools requires an offbeat form, you will have it.

WHEN TO APPLY?

How about Christmas Eve? That's probably not a good time to pore over numbers but by then your forms should be in hand and getting some serious thought.

The ideal time to sit down for two or three hours and fill in little boxes is the last week of the year, December 26–31. It's ideal because school is out and daily requirements of homework and school activities have subsided. You have fewer conflicting demands on your time.

It's ideal also because federal law requires financial aid applications to be submitted after January 1. That means on January 2, the early birds will be at their post offices with applications. Join the early birds. It can give you a distinct advantage over those who wait.

The pot of available money is finite. It runs out. Students first in line have the satisfaction of knowing their applications will be considered solely on their merits, not rejected because a school has spent all its cash.

STEPS ALONG THE WAY

A checklist to prepare for college and pay for it:

8th Grade

—Find out what courses you should take in high school to best prepare you for college.

—Get a Social Security number if you don't have one.

9th Grade

—Look into career information in areas that match your interests and abilities.

—Talk to school counselor about your future, what colleges might best serve you and what they might cost. Take your parents along.

—Work with your parents to establish a plan to finance college.

10th Grade

—Write to colleges for catalogs/brochures to get an idea of their offerings, admission requirements, financial aid policies.

—Take the PSAT to prepare for college admission tests.

11th Grade/Fall

—Think about a college major if you haven't decided on one.

—Attend college fairs, meet with college representatives who visit your school to talk about specific colleges.

—Make a list of colleges that interest you. Write for their admission/financial aid information.

—Take PSAT to prepare for college admission tests, establish eligibility for National Merit Scholarship.

—Talk to your counselor about your PSAT scores and their implications for your college career.

—Visit a library at school, in your community or at a nearby college to research lists of private scholarships for which you might qualify.

11th Grade/Spring

—Take the SAT or ACT depending on which is required by the colleges that interest you. If your colleges ask for Achievement Tests, take them.

—Narrow your list of colleges and make plans to visit them. Write for an appointment at the admission office. Allow time to talk to students, professors.

—Write to organizations on your private scholarship list requesting information.

—Develop a resume of high school activities and awards that you can update as necessary.

—Find a summer job.

11th Grade/Summer

—Request admission, financial aid forms from the colleges to which you intend to apply.

Some colleges will ask you to submit a PROFILE in the fall of your senior year so they can get a head start processing your data. Those that want it early will let you know.

"We have a certain percentage every year who don't submit [aid

STEPS ALONG THE WAY
(continued)

12th Grade/Fall

—Make sure you're taking courses to meet the requirements of colleges to which you're applying.

—Take the SAT or ACT again. Most colleges will consider only your highest score.

—Attend college fairs, meet with college representatives.

—Apply for private scholarships for which you're eligible.

—Think about your application essay. Talk to your counselor and English teacher about it.

—Ask teachers to write recommendations for you. The number each college requests will be in its application material.

12th Grade/Winter

—Apply to colleges of your choice by their deadlines.

—Work with your parents to collect financial information. Submit financial aid application as soon as possible after January 1.

—Ask your counselor if a separate application is needed for your state's financial aid. If so, submit it.

—Respond immediately to any request for more information or additional documents in your financial aid application.

—Be sure your high school sends a transcript to colleges where you have applied.

—Call the organizations where you've applied for private scholarships to ask how you're doing.

12th Grade/Spring

—After you get letters of acceptance and financial aid awards, decide which college you will attend. Accept its offer by its deadline or the spot may go to someone else. Decline other offers in writing.

—Review the financial aid package with your parents. Be sure you understand each kind of aid offered to you. Schedule an appointment with the school's financial aid director if you have questions.

—Sign the financial aid award letter and return it by the deadline.

—Notify the financial aid office of the private scholarships you are receiving.

—Complete any separate applications for loans you decide to accept.

—Find a summer job.

Source: National Association of Student Financial Aid Administrators

applications] early enough," says Ron Shunk, financial aid director at Gettysburg College. "They will get admitted [to the college] but they will have to sit and wait until we get their information and see if we have enough aid." If a student applies early, says Shunk, a financial aid letter will be in the mail within 10 days of the acceptance letter from the admission office.

WHERE ARE THE NUMBERS?

Much of the information requested by the two basic forms comes from the student's and/or parents' tax returns. The information they want is on the returns due April 15 of the year you're applying—three months after the ideal time to apply for financial aid.

In the last week of 1995, you probably won't have all the precise numbers needed for your tax return due in April 1996. For example, the W-2 forms from your employers have not yet arrived, nor have the notices from the bank reporting how much interest you've earned. In order to get your financial aid request in early you will have to estimate. Be sure to check the box at the top of the request form that says that you are estimating so that the college is aware of what you are doing. The college may ask for verification at a later time.

Even if you're uncomfortable guessing, do it. If you make a significant mistake with an estimate, you can correct it on a form you'll later get in the mail. Don't sacrifice a timely aid application for the sake of precise numbers. Otherwise, come April, you could be in the group that sits and waits.

Now let's take a stroll through the forms themselves, reproduced here.

THE FAFSA

Be careful. Answer every question that pertains to you regardless of how innocuous it appears. If an answer is zero, write "0." An empty space can trigger a computer's request for more information that can stall your application for a month.

Filling out the FAFSA starts easy. Sections A, B, and C just want your vital statistics. A key item in Section B is the question asking what types of financial aid you will accept. Check all the boxes. Even if you don't want a Work-Study job, check it. Financial aid directors are more amenable to students who are

Free Application for Federal Student Aid

WARNING: If you purposely give false or misleading information on this form, you may be fined $10,000, sent to prison, or both.

"You" and "your" on this form always mean the student who wants aid.

F F F F F

Form Approved
OMB No. 1840-0110
APP. EXP. 6/30/97

U.S. Department of Education
Student Financial
Assistance Programs

Section A: Yourself

1–3. Your name

1. Last **2.** First **3.** M.I.

Your title (optional) Mr. ☐ ₁ Miss, Ms., or Mrs. ☐ ₂

4–7. Your permanent mailing address
(*All mail will be sent to this address. See Instructions, page 2 for state/country abbreviations.*)

4. Number and street (Include apt. no.)

5. City **6.** State **7.** ZIP code

8. Your permanent home telephone number Area code

9. Your state of legal residence State

10. Date you became a legal resident of the state in question 9 (*See Instructions, page 2.*) Month Day Year

11–12. Your driver's license number (*Include the state abbreviation. If you don't have a license, leave this question blank.*)
State

13. Your social security number (*Don't leave blank. See Instructions, page 3.*)

14. Your date of birth Month Day Year

15–16. Are you a U.S. citizen? (*See Instructions, page 3.*)
Yes, I am a U.S. citizen. ☐ ₁
No, but I am an eligible noncitizen. ☐ ₂
A
No, neither of the above. ☐ ₃

17. As of **today**, are you married? (*Check only one box.*)
I am not married. (I am single, widowed, or divorced.) ☐ ₁
I am married. ☐ ₂
I am separated from my spouse. ☐ ₃

18. Date you were married, widowed, separated, or divorced. If divorced, use earliest date of divorce or separation. Month Year

19. Will you have your first bachelor's degree before July 1, 1996? Yes ☐ ₁ No ☐ ₂

Section B: Your Plans

20. Your year in college during the 1996–97 school year (*Check only one box.*)
1st ☐ ₁ 3rd ☐ ₃ 5th year or more undergraduate ☐ ₅
2nd ☐ ₂ 4th ☐ ₄ graduate ☐ ₆

21–24. Your expected enrollment status for the 1996–97 school year (*See Instructions, page 3.*)

School term	Full time	3/4 time	1/2 time	Less than 1/2 time	Not enrolled
21. Summer term '96	☐ ₁	☐ ₂	☐ ₃	☐ ₄	☐ ₅
22. Fall sem./quarter '96	☐ ₁	☐ ₂	☐ ₃	☐ ₄	☐ ₅
23. Winter quarter '96–'97	☐ ₁	☐ ₂	☐ ₃	☐ ₄	☐ ₅
24. Spring sem./quarter '97	☐ ₁	☐ ₂	☐ ₃	☐ ₄	☐ ₅

25–26. Your degree/certificate and course of study (*See Instructions, page 3.*)
25. Degree/certificate
26. Course of study

27. Date you expect to complete your degree/certificate Month Day Year

28–30. In addition to grants, what other types of financial aid are you (and your parents) interested in? (*Check one or more boxes.*)
• Work-study ☐ ₁
• Student loans ☐ ₂
• Parent loans for students (Federal PLUS) ☐ ₃

31. If you are (or were) in college, do you plan to attend **that same college** in 1996–97?
Yes ☐ ₁ No ☐ ₂

32. For how many dependent children will you pay child care expenses in 1996–97?

33–34. Veterans education benefits you expect to receive from July 1, 1996, through June 30, 1997
33. Amount per month $_____ .00
34. Number of months

Section C: Education Background   *Page 2*

35–36. Date that you (the student) received, or will
receive, your high school diploma, either—

- by graduating from high school

  OR

  |___|___| |___|___|___|
  Month   Year

- by earning a GED

  |___|___| |___|___|___|
  Month   Year

  *(Enter **one** date. Leave blank if the question
  does not apply to you.)*

37–38. Highest grade level completed by your father and
your mother *(Check one box for each parent.
See Instructions, page 4.)*

	37. Father	38. Mother
elementary school (K–8)	☐1	☐1
high school (9–12)	☐2	☐2
college or beyond	☐3	☐3
unknown	☐4	☐4

Section D: Federal Family Education Loan (FFEL) Program Information

*(Leave this section blank if you have never received a Federal Stafford Loan, a guaranteed student loan [GSL], or
a Federal Insured Student Loan [FISL].)*

39. If you borrowed under the Federal Stafford, Federal SLS,
Federal PLUS, or Federal Consolidation Loan program and
there is an outstanding balance on your loan(s), enter the date
of your oldest outstanding loan.

|___|___| |___|___|
Month   Year

42. Check one box to indicate the interest rate you have
on your outstanding Federal Stafford Loan.

7% ☐1   9% ☐3   Variable ☐5

8% ☐2   8%/10% ☐4

40–41. Write in the total outstanding balance(s) on your
Federal Stafford and Federal SLS Loans.

Amount owed

40. Federal Stafford Loan(s) $_____.00

41. Federal SLS Loan(s) $_____.00

43–44. Do you currently have a Federal PLUS Loan or a
Consolidation Loan?

	Yes	No
43. Federal PLUS Loan	☐1	☐2
44. Federal Consolidation Loan	☐1	☐2

Section E: Student Status

	Yes	No
45. Were you born **before** January 1, 1973?	☐1	☐2
46. Are you a veteran of the U.S. Armed Forces?	☐1	☐2
47. Will you be a graduate or professional student in 1996–97?	☐1	☐2
48. Are you married?	☐1	☐2
49. Are you a ward of the court or are both your parents dead?	☐1	☐2
50. Do you have legal dependents (*other than a spouse*) that fit the definition in Instructions, page 4?	☐1	☐2

If you answered **"Yes"** to **any** question in Section
E, go to Section F and fill out the **GRAY** and the
WHITE areas on the rest of the form.

If you answered **"No"** to **every** question in Section
E, go to Section F, and fill out the **BLUE**
and the **WHITE** areas on the rest of the form.

Section F: Household Information

**If you are filling out the GRAY and WHITE areas,
answer questions 51 and 52, and go to Section G.**

**If you are filling out the BLUE and WHITE areas, skip
questions 51 and 52. Answer questions 53 through 57
about your parents, and then go on to Section G.**

STUDENT (& SPOUSE)

51. Number of family members in 1996–97
(Include yourself and your spouse.
Include your children and other people only if
they meet the definition in Instructions,
page 5.) |___|

52. Number of college students in 1996–97
(Of the number in 51, how many will be in
college at least half-time for at least one term?
Include yourself. *See Instructions, page 5.*) |___|

PARENTS

53. Your parents' current marital status:

single ☐1   separated ☐3   widowed ☐5

married ☐2   divorced ☐4

54. Your parents' state of legal residence |___|

55. Date your parent(s) became legal resident(s)
of the state in question 54
(See Instructions, page 5.)

|___|___| |___|___| |___|___|
Month   Day   Year

56. Number of family members in 1996–97
(Include yourself and your parents. Include your parents'
other children and other people only if they meet the
definition in Instructions, page 5.) |___|

57. Number of college students in 1996–97
(Of the number in 56, how many will be in college at
least half-time for at least one term? Include yourself.
See Instructions, page 6.) |___|

Section G: 1995 Income, Earnings, and Benefits

Everyone must fill out the Student (& Spouse) column. *Page 3*

(You must see the instructions for income and taxes that you should exclude from questions in this section.)

STUDENT (& SPOUSE)

58. The following 1995 U.S. income tax figures are from:
(Check only one box.)

a completed 1995 IRS Form 1040A or 1040EZ   (Go to 59) ☐₁

a completed 1995 IRS Form 1040   (Go to 59) ☐₂

an estimated 1995 IRS Form 1040A or 1040EZ   (Go to 59) ☐₃

an estimated 1995 IRS Form 1040   (Go to 59) ☐₄

A U.S. income tax return will not be filed.   (Skip to 62) ☐₅

PARENTS

69. The following 1995 U.S. income tax figures are from:
(Check only one box.)

a completed 1995 IRS Form 1040A or 1040EZ   (Go to 70) ☐₁

a completed 1995 IRS Form 1040   (Go to 70) ☐₂

an estimated 1995 IRS Form 1040A or 1040EZ   (Go to 70) ☐₃

an estimated 1995 IRS Form 1040   (Go to 70) ☐₄

A U.S. income tax return will not be filed.   (Skip to 73) ☐₅

	STUDENT (& SPOUSE)		PARENTS
1995 total number of exemptions (Form 1040-line 6e, or 1040A-line 6e; 1040EZ filers—*see Instructions, pages 6 & 7.*)	**59.** ⊔⊔		**70.** ⊔⊔
1995 Adjusted Gross Income (AGI-Form 1040-line 31, 1040A-line 16, or 1040EZ-line 4, or *see Instructions, pages 6 & 7.*)	**60.** $_____.00	— TAX FILERS ONLY —	**71.** $_____.00
1995 U.S. income tax paid (Form 1040-line 46, 1040A-line 25, or 1040EZ-line 8)	**61.** $_____.00		**72.** $_____.00
1995 Income earned from work Student	**62.** $_____.00	Father	**73.** $_____.00
1995 Income earned from work Spouse	**63.** $_____.00	Mother	**74.** $_____.00

1995 Untaxed income and benefits (yearly totals only)

Social security benefits	**64.** $_____.00		**75.** $_____.00
Aid to Families with Dependent Children (AFDC or ADC)	**65.** $_____.00		**76.** $_____.00
Child support received for all children	**66.** $_____.00		**77.** $_____.00
Other untaxed income and benefits from Worksheet #2, page 11	**67.** $_____.00		**78.** $_____.00
1995 Title IV Income Exclusions from Worksheet #3, page 12	**68.** $_____.00		**79.** $_____.00

Section H: Information Release

80-91. What college(s) do you plan to attend in 1996–97?
*(**Note:** By answering this question, you are giving permission to send your application data to the college(s) you list below.)*

Housing codes	1 = on-campus	3 = with parent(s)
	2 = off-campus	4 = with relative(s) other than parent(s)

	College name	Address (or code, see Instructions, page 7)	City	State	Housing codes
80.	_____	_____	_____	___	**81.**
82.	_____	_____	_____	___	**83.**
84.	_____	_____	_____	___	**85.**
86.	_____	_____	_____	___	**87.**
88.	_____	_____	_____	___	**89.**
90.	_____	_____	_____	___	**91.**

92. Do you give the U.S. Department of Education permission to send information from this form to the financial aid agencies in your state as well as to the state agencies of all of the colleges listed above?   Yes ☐₁ No ☐₂

(States and colleges may require additional information and may have their own deadlines for applying for financial aid. Be sure to see "Deadlines for State Student Aid" in Instructions, page 10.)

93. Check this box if you give Selective Service permission to register you. *(See Instructions, page 8.)*   ☐₁

94–95. Read and Sign   *Page 4*

Certification: All of the information provided by me or any other person on this form and in Section I, if completed, is true and complete to the best of my knowledge. I understand that this application is being filed jointly by all signatories. If asked by an authorized official, I agree to give proof of the information that I have given on this form and in Section I, if completed. I realize that this proof may include a copy of my U.S., state, or local income tax return. I also realize that if I do not give proof when asked, the student may be denied aid.

94. Everyone giving information on this form must sign below.
    If you do not sign this form, it will be returned unprocessed.

1 Student _____

2 Student's spouse _____

3 Father/Stepfather _____

4 Mother/Stepmother _____

95. Date completed   Month   Day   Year   1996 ☐   1997 ☐

School Use Only

Dependency override: enter I ☐

Title IV Inst. Number _____

FAA signature: I _____

MDE Use Only   Spec.   No.
(Do not write in this box.)   handle ☐   copies ☐

If you (and your family) have unusual circumstances, such as:

- tuition expenses at an elementary or secondary school,
- unusual medical or dental expenses, not covered by insurance,
- a family member who is a dislocated worker, or
- other unusual circumstances that might affect your eligibility for student financial aid, you should—
    Check with the financial aid office at your college.

Preparer's Use Only   *(For preparers other than student and parents. Student and parents, sign above. See Instructions, page 8.)*

Preparer's name

_____
Last   First   M.I.

Firm's name and address (or preparer's, if self-employed)

_____
Firm name

_____
Number and street (Include apt. no.)

_____
City   State   ZIP code

96. Employer identification
    number (EIN) _____

97. Preparer's social
    security number _____

Certification:
All of the information on this form and in Section I, if completed, is true and complete to the best of my knowledge.

98. Preparer's signature   Date

--- ATTENTION ---

If you are filling out the GRAY and WHITE areas, go to Instructions, page 8, and complete WORKSHEET A. This will tell you whether you must fill out Section I. If you meet certain tax filing and income conditions, you may skip Section I.

If you are filling out the BLUE and WHITE areas, go to Instructions, page 8, and complete WORKSHEET B. This will tell you whether you must fill out Section I. If you meet certain tax filing and income conditions, you may skip Section I.

Section I: Asset Information

	STUDENT (& SPOUSE)	PARENTS
		106. Age of your older parent ☐☐
Cash, savings, and checking accounts	**99.** $_____.00	**107.** $_____.00
Other real estate and investments value *(Don't include the home.)*	**100.** $_____.00	**108.** $_____.00
Other real estate and investments debt *(Don't include the home.)*	**101.** $_____.00	**109.** $_____.00
Business value	**102.** $_____.00	**110.** $_____.00
Business debt	**103.** $_____.00	**111.** $_____.00
Farm value *(See Instructions, pages 8 & 9.)*	**104.** $_____.00	**112.** $_____.00
Farm debt *(See Instructions, pages 8 & 9.)*	**105.** $_____.00	**113.** $_____.00

MAKE SURE THAT YOU HAVE COMPLETED, DATED, AND SIGNED THE APPLICATION.
Mail the application to: Federal Student Aid Programs, P.O. Box 4016, Iowa City, IA 52243-4016.

flexible. If you don't like the aid package eventually offered, you can decline parts of it or renegotiate the package.

Section D can be ignored by first-time applicants. It's only for students who have received a federally guaranteed college loan in the past. Sort of a credit record.

The six questions in Section E are the same six you read in Chapter Two, determining if your parents must provide financial information. Answer one of the six "yes" and you're officially independent. Your spouse, if you have one, must disclose his or her financial condition, but your parents need not. If all six answers are "no," you are considered dependent, and your parents must report.

Thousands of early birds estimate the numbers. That's why they are early birds. Join them.

In Section F, which looks fairly routine, is a box that can significantly effect your magic number and your aid package. It's the last question, which asks the number of family members who will be in college "at least half-time for at least one term."

The higher the number you put in that box, the greater your Need will be. Remember the formula for Expected Family Contribution. The last step, after determining your EFC, is to divide it by the number of family members in college.

If the formula says your EFC is $6,000, and you have a "2" in that Sec-

Answer all questions, even those that get answered with a "0."

tion F box, it becomes $3,000. If you report "3" family members in college, your EFC is $2,000, and your magic number climbs.

Don't stretch the truth, of course, but be aware of what the form is asking. A half-time student, by FAFSA definition, is anyone carrying six credits at an accredited four- or two-year institution. If your mother has been thinking about taking a couple of classes at the community college, now is the time

Keep your options open: check all types of aid.

Above all, be honest when filling out the forms.

to do it. You can count her as a family member in college. You could recoup more than the cost of her tuition in your own financial aid.

The financial soul-baring begins in Section G. The questions are straightforward and easy to understand. How much did you, your spouse, and parents make last year from work and investments? How much do you have in the bank? The answers, especially if you are estimating in late December, might take some time to find.

Don't grossly underestimate your income in the hope that an unknowing computer will give you a break on an EFC. That can backfire with devastating consequences if you are asked to submit your records for verification. Financial aid directors, as we'll see in the next chapter, have great flexibility in dispensing aid money, even in government programs. A financial aid director is to be cultivated as a friend. Underreporting income is not a good way to start.

THE PROFILE

PROFILE is a newcomer to the financial aid family, arriving in the fall of 1995. It replaces the venerable FAF, which had been used in recent years as a supplement to the federal form by colleges that want more information. While the FAF asked questions that aren't on the FAFSA, PROFILE covers the same ground as the FAFSA and then asks more. That helps colleges who want to estimate your EFC early to get all the information they need before your FAFSA is processed.

To get a copy of the PROFILE, you must send The College Board a one-page registration sheet that provides your vital statistics such as name, address, and Social Security number. You also need to list the colleges that should receive your PROFILE information. By the time you read this, well-equipped high school guidance offices should have a supply of registration forms.

The PROFILE you receive will contain four or five pages. The first four pages ask for information that goes to every college. If you get a fifth page, it means some colleges on your list want to know even more. Page five contains questions that individual schools want the PROFILE to ask. Each question on page five will identify the college asking it.

When you fill out the PROFILE, take care to answer all pertinent questions even with a zero. As with the FAFSA, unanswered questions will send the form back to you, delaying the process.

When you start putting numbers on the form, be careful! The PROFILE asks many of the same questions about you and your parents as the FAFSA. Be sure you have the same numbers—for income, assets, taxes, etc.—on each form. Different answers to the same questions will be noticed by a computer somewhere. And you will be asked to explain the difference.

Don't forget to include medical and dental expenses (if when totaled they are greater than 4 percent of your income) on the PROFILE.

The PROFILE, however, wants to know more about your financial condition than the FAFSA. Some of the additional information could give you a break. Most of it won't.

The first available break is at the bottom of page one in the section on the student's expenses. One question asks about your medical and dental expenses not covered by insurance. If you have any unreimbursed medical or dental bills, add them up and report the total. If it's more than 4 percent of your income, the total will be deducted from your income when the formula figures your EFC, a break not available on the FAFSA.

A similar break for your parents comes on page two. They are asked about unreimbursed medical or dental expenses and about child support payments, their own college loans, and tuition paid for your siblings. Those expenses also will be deducted from income in calculating your EFC.

The two reasons most colleges want the PROFILE in addition to the FAFSA are at the bottom of pages two and three. On page two, parents are asked to report assets including their home, which the FAFSA spe-

Financial Aid *P*ROFILE — 1996-97

Complete all sections of the PROFILE Form except Section E. Be certain that everyone giving information on the form signs it.

Section A — Student's Information

1. How many family members will the student (and spouse) support in 1996-97? List their names and give information about them in M. See instructions. ☐

2. Of the number in 1, how many will be in college at least half-time for at least one term in 1996-97? Include yourself. ☐☐

3. What is the student's state of legal residence? ☐☐

4. What is the student's citizenship status?

a. ₁☐ U.S. citizen

   ₂☐ Permanent resident

   ₃☐ Neither of the above (Answer "b" and "c" below.)

b. Country of citizenship?

☐☐☐☐☐☐☐☐☐☐☐☐☐☐☐☐☐

c. Visa classification?

₁☐ F1   ₂☐ F2   ₃☐ J1   ₄☐ J2   ₅☐ Other

Section B — Student's 1995 Income & Benefits

Don't report parents' information on this page. If married, include spouse's information in Sections B, C, D, and E.

Tax Filers Only

5. The following 1995 U.S. Income tax return figures are (Mark only one box.)

₁☐ estimated. Will file IRS Form 1040EZ or 1040A. Go to 6.

₂☐ estimated. Will file IRS Form 1040. Go to 6.

₃☐ from a completed IRS Form 1040EZ or 1040A. Go to 6.

₄☐ from a completed IRS Form 1040. Go to 6.

₅☐ a tax return will not be filed. Skip to 10.

6. 1995 total number of exemptions (IRS Form 1040, line 6e or 1040A, line 6e or 1040EZ — see instructions) **6.** ☐☐

7. 1995 Adjusted Gross Income from IRS Form 1040, line 31 or 1040A, line 13 or 1040EZ, line 3 (Use the worksheet in the instructions.) **7.** $_____ .00

8. 1995 U.S. income tax paid (IRS Form 1040, line 47 or 1040A, line 22 or 1040EZ, line 9) **8.** $_____ .00

9. 1995 itemized deductions (IRS Form 1040, Schedule A, line 26. Write in "0" if deductions were not itemized.) **9.** $_____ .00

10. 1995 income earned from work by student (See instructions.) **10.** $_____ .00

11. 1995 income earned from work by student's spouse **11.** $_____ .00

12. 1995 dividend and interest income **12.** $_____ .00

13. 1995 untaxed income and benefits (Give total amount for the year.)

a. Social security benefits (See instructions.) **13. a.** $_____ .00

b. Aid to Families with Dependent Children **b.** $_____ .00

c. Child support received for all the student's children **c.** $_____ .00

d. Earned Income Credit (IRS Form 1040, line 56 or 1040A, line 28c) **d.** $_____ .00

e. Other – write total from worksheet, page X. **e.** $_____ .00

14. 1995 earnings from Federal Work-Study or other need-based work programs plus any grant and scholarship aid in excess of tuition, fees, books, and supplies **14.** $_____ .00

Section C — Student's Assets

15. Cash, savings, and checking accounts $_____ .00

	What is it worth today?	What is owed on it?

16. Investments (Including Uniform Gifts to Minors. See instructions.) $_____ .00 $_____ .00

17. Home (Renters write in "0.") $_____ .00 $_____ .00

18. Other real estate $_____ .00 $_____ .00

19. Business and farm $_____ .00 $_____ .00

20. If the farm is included in 19, is the student living on the farm? Yes ☐₁ No ☐₂

21. If student owns home, give

a. year purchased ☐1☐9☐☐   b. purchase price $_____ .00

Section D — Student's Trust Information

22. a. Total value of all trust(s) $_____ .00

b. Is any income or part of the principal currently available? Yes ☐₁ No ☐₂

c. Who established the trust(s)?

₁☐ Student's parents   ₂☐ Other

Section E — Student's Expenses

23. 1995 child support paid by student $_____ .00

24. 1995 medical and dental expenses not covered by insurance (See instructions.) $_____ .00

Section F — Student's Expected Summer/School-Year Resources for 1996-97

	Amount per month	Number of months
25. Student's veterans benefits (July 1, 1996 – June 30, 1997)	$ .00	└┴┘

26. Student's (and spouse's) resources
(Don't enter monthly amounts.)

	Summer 1996 (3 months)	School Year 1996-97 (9 months)
a. Student's wages, salaries, tips, etc.	$ .00	$ .00
b. Spouse's wages, salaries, tips, etc.	$ .00	$ .00
c. Other taxable income	$ .00	$ .00
d. Untaxed income and benefits	$ .00	$ .00
e. Grants, scholarships, fellowships, etc. from other than the colleges to which the student is applying (List sources in Section P.)		$ .00
f. Tuition benefits from the parents' and/or the student's or spouse's employer		$ .00
g. Contributions from the student's parent(s)		$ .00
h. Contributions from other relatives, spouse's parents, and all other sources		$ .00

Section G — Parents' Household Information – See page X of the instruction booklet.

27. How many family members will your parents support in 1996-97? <u>Always include yourself (the student)</u>. List their names and give information about them in M. └┴┘

28. Of the number in 27, how many will be in college at least half-time for at least one term in 1996-97? Include the student. └─┘

29. How many parents will be in college at least half-time in 1996-97? (Mark only one box.)

1 ☐ Neither parent   2 ☐ One parent   3 ☐ Both parents

30. What is the current marital status of your parents? (Mark only one box.)

1 ☐ single   3 ☐ separated   5 ☐ widowed
2 ☐ married   4 ☐ divorced

31. What is your parents' state of legal residence? └┴┘

Section H — Parents' Expenses

	1995	Expected 1996
32. Child support paid by the parent(s) completing this form	32 a. $ .00	32. b. $ .00
33. Repayment of educational loans (See instructions.)	33 a. $ .00	33. b. $ .00
34. Medical and dental expenses not covered by insurance (See instructions.)	34 a. $ .00	34. b. $ .00

35. Total elementary, junior high school, and high school tuition paid for dependent children

	1995	Expected 1996
Amount paid (Don't include tuition paid for the student.)	35 a. $ .00	35c. $ .00
For how many dependent children? (Don't include the student.)	b. └─┘	d. └─┘

Section I — Parents' Assets – If parents own all or part of a business or farm, write in its name and the percent of ownership in Section P.

	What is it worth today?	What is owed on it?
36. Cash, savings, and checking accounts $ .00		
37. Monthly home mortgage or rental payment (If none, explain in Section P.) $ .00		
40. Business	$ .00	$ .00
41. a. Farm	$ .00	$ .00

	What is it worth today?	What is owed on it?
38. Investments	$ .00	$ .00
39a. Home (Renters write in "0.")	$ .00	$ .00

b. year purchased |1|9| | c. purchase price $ .00

41. b. Does family live on the farm?

Yes ☐ 1   No ☐ 2

42. a. Other real estate $ .00 $ .00

b. year purchased |1|9| | c. purchase price $ .00

*P*ROFILE — 1996-97

Section J — Parents' 1994 Income and Benefits

43. 1994 Adjusted Gross Income (IRS Form 1040, line 31 or 1040A, line 13 or 1040EZ, line 3)　$ _____ .00

44. 1994 U.S. Income tax paid (IRS Form 1040, line 47, 1040A, line 22 or 1040EZ, line 9)　$ _____ .00

45. 1994 itemized deductions (IRS Form 1040, Schedule A, line 26. Write "0" if deductions were not itemized)　$ _____ .00

46. 1994 untaxed income and benefits (Include the same types of income & benefits that are listed in 53 a – k.)　$ _____ .00

Section K — Parents' 1995 Income & Benefits

47. The following 1995 U.S. income tax return figures are (Mark only one box.)

1 ☐ estimated. Will file IRS Form 1040EZ or 1040A. Go to 48.　2 ☐ estimated. Will file IRS Form 1040. Go to 48.　3 ☐ from a completed IRS Form 1040EZ or 1040A. Go to 48.　4 ☐ from a completed IRS Form 1040. Go to 48.　5 ☐ a tax return will not be filed. Skip to 52.

48. 1995 total number of exemptions (IRS Form 1040, line 6e or 1040A, line 6e or 1040EZ)　**48.** ☐☐

49. 1995 Adjusted Gross Income (IRS Form 1040, line 31 or 1040A, line 13 or 1040EZ, line 3)　**49.** $ _____ .00

Breakdown of income in 49

a. Wages, salaries, tips (IRS Form 1040, line 7 or 1040A, line 7 or 1040EZ, line 1)　49 a. $ _____ .00

b. Interest income (IRS Form 1040, line 8a or 1040A, line 8a or 1040EZ, line 2)　b. $ _____ .00

c. Dividend income (IRS Form 1040, line 9 or 1040A, line 9)　c. $ _____ .00

d. Net income (or loss) from business, farm, rents, royalties, partnerships, estates, trusts, etc. (IRS Form 1040, lines 12, 18, and 19) If a loss, enter the amount in (parentheses).　d. $ _____ .00

e. Other taxable income such as alimony received, capital gains (or losses), pensions, annuities, etc. (IRS Form 1040, lines 10, 11, 13-15, 16b, 17b, 20, 21b, and 22 or 1040A, line 10)　e. $ _____ .00

f. Adjustments to income (IRS Form 1040, line 30 or 1040A, line 12c)　f. $ _____ .00

50. 1995 U.S. income tax paid (IRS Form 1040, line 47, 1040A, line 22 or 1040EZ, line 9)　**50.** $ _____ .00

51. 1995 itemized deductions (IRS Form 1040, Schedule A, line 26. Write in "0" if deductions were not itemized.)　**51.** $ _____ .00

Tax Filers Only

52. 1995 Income earned from work by father　**52.** $ _____ .00

53. 1995 Income earned from work by mother　**53.** $ _____ .00

54. 1995 untaxed income and benefits (Give total amount for the year. Do not give monthly amounts.)

a. Social security benefits　**54a.** $ _____ .00

b. Aid to Families with Dependent Children　b. $ _____ .00

c. Child support received for all children　c. $ _____ .00

d. Deductible IRA and/or Keogh payments (See instructions.)　d. $ _____ .00

e. Payments to tax-deferred pension and savings plans (See instructions.)　e. $ _____ .00

f. Amounts withheld from wages for dependent care and medical spending accounts　f. $ _____ .00

g. Earned Income Credit (IRS Form 1040, line 56 or 1040A, line 28c)　g. $ _____ .00

h. Housing, food and other living allowances (See instructions.)　h. $ _____ .00

i. Tax-exempt interest income (IRS Form 1040, line 8b or 1040A, line 8b)　i. $ _____ .00

j. Foreign income exclusion (IRS Form 2555, line 43)　j. $ _____ .00

k. Other – write in the total from the worksheet in the instructions, page X.　k. $ _____ .00

WRITE ONLY IN THE ANSWER SPACES. DO NOT WRITE ANYWHERE ELSE.

Section L — Parents' 1996 Expected Income & Benefits

(If the expected total income and benefits will differ from the 1995 total income and benefits by $3,000 or more, explain in P.)

55. 1996 income earned from work by father　$ _____ .00　**57.** 1996 other taxable income　$ _____ .00

56. 1996 income earned from work by mother　$ _____ .00　**58.** 1996 untaxed income and benefits　$ _____ .00

Section M —Family Member Listing
– Give information for all family members but don't give information about yourself. List up to seven other family members here. If there are more than seven, list first those who will be in college at least half-time. List the others in Section P.

59.

Full name of family member	Age	Claimed as tax exemption in 1995? Yes? No?	*Use codes from below.	1995-96 school year				1996-97 school year		
You — the student applicant				Name of school or college	Year in school	Scholarships and grants	Parents' contri- bution	Attend college at least one term full-time half-time		Name of school or college
1										
2		☐ ☐						₁☐ ₂☐		
3		☐ ☐						₁☐ ₂☐		
4		☐ ☐						₁☐ ₂☐		
5		☐ ☐						₁☐ ₂☐		
6		☐ ☐						₁☐ ₂☐		
7		☐ ☐						₁☐ ₂☐		
8		☐ ☐						₁☐ ₂☐		

Write in the correct code from the right. ↑   1 = Student's parent 3 = Student's brother or sister 5 = Student's son or daughter 7 = Other
2 = Student's stepparent 4 = Student's husband or wife 6 = Student's grandparent

Section N — Parents' Information

60. Mark one: ☐ Father ☐ Stepfather ☐ Legal guardian ☐ Other (Explain in P.)

a. Name _____ Age ☐☐

b. Mark if: ☐ Self-employed ☐ Unemployed – Date last employed: _____

c. Occupation _____

d. Employer _____ No. years _____

e. Work telephone (optional) ☐☐☐-☐☐☐-☐☐☐☐

f. Retirement plans: ☐ Social security ☐ Union/employer ☐ Civil service/state ☐ IRA/Keogh/tax-deferred ☐ Military ☐ Other

61. Mark one: ☐ Mother ☐ Stepmother ☐ Legal guardian ☐ Other (Explain in P.)

a. Name _____ Age ☐☐

b. Mark if: ☐ Self-employed ☐ Unemployed – Date last employed: _____

c. Occupation _____

d. Employer _____ No. years _____

e. Work telephone (optional) ☐☐☐-☐☐☐-☐☐☐☐

f. Retirement plans: ☐ Social security only ☐ Union/employer ☐ Civil service/state ☐ IRA/Keogh/tax-deferred ☐ Military ☐ Other

Section O — Divorced, Separated, or Remarried Parents
(To be answered by the parent who completes this form, if the student's natural or adoptive parents are divorced, separated, or remarried.)

62. a. Year of separation ☐☐   Year of divorce ☐☐

b. Other parent's name _____

Home address _____

_____

Occupation/Employer _____

c. According to court order, when will support for the student end? ☐☐ ☐☐ Month Year

d. Who last claimed the student as a tax exemption? _____

_____ Year? ☐☐

e. How much does the other parent plan to contribute to the student's education for the 1995-96 school year? $ _____ .00

f. Is there an agreement specifying this contribution for the student's education? Yes ☐ No ☐

Section P — Explanations/Special Circumstances
Use this space to explain any unusual expenses such as high medical or dental expenses, educational and other debts, child care, elder care, or special circumstances. Also, give information for any outside scholarships you have been awarded.

Certification:
All the information on this form is true and complete to the best of my knowledge. If asked, I agree to give proof of the information that I have given on this form. I realize that this proof may include a copy of my U.S., state, or local income tax returns. I certify that all information is correct at this time, and that I will send timely notice of any significant change in family income or assets, financial situation, college plans of other children, or the receipt of other scholarships or grants.

1 _____
Student's signature

2 _____
Student's spouse's signature

3 _____
Father's (stepfather's) signature

4 _____
Mother's (stepmother's) signature

Date this form was completed:
☐☐ ☐☐ ☐☐ ₁☐ 1995 ₂☐ 1996 ₃☐ 1997
Month Day Year

cifically excludes. The debate over home equity as a factor in Expected Family Contribution is described in Chapter Two and it continues to rage. This is where the colleges that want it, get it.

On page three, parents estimate their coming year's income. That could give the student a break if a parent lost a job or has moved to a lower-paying position. A sympathetic financial aid director can consider estimated current income instead of last year's earnings.

On page four, the PROFILE wants the names of your family members who are attending college, just to be sure you're not imagining a few.

If you are officially dependent and your parents are divorced or separated, the PROFILE wants some information about the noncustodial parent and any support he or she is providing. (The PROFILE already knows if your parents are divorced or separated because you answered the question on your registration form.) Some colleges will insist that the noncustodial parent submit a separate financial disclosure form. If such a college is on your list, the separate form will be included with your PROFILE.

William Miller, head of the College Scholarship Service that provides the PROFILE and other forms, says the Divorced/Separated Parents' Statement is used only for colleges that request it. "Colleges that want to use them want very much to use them," says Miller. "Those that don't feel very strongly that they don't want them."

DON'T FORGET TO SIGN!

The No. 1 reason that financial aid applications are returned to senders is a missing signature.

All who submit information on the FAFSA—student, parents, spouse—must sign. And the form makes it easy to forget, asking for signatures in the upper-left corner of the last page. (The PROFILE is signed in the customary place, the end.)

Don't forget. Sign it.

NOW WHAT HAPPENS?

Within four weeks after you mail your FAFSA, you'll get a response from the U.S. Department of Education. It will contain either:

1. A request for more information.
2. Your Expected Family Contribution, the key to finding your magic number.

You don't want No. 1. A request for more information means you weren't careful enough filling out your form. It could be—and often is—something as simple as a failure to sign your name. It could be that you report two siblings but neglect to put a number in the little box that says how many family members are in college. Or it could be something significant like your father refused to list his assets.

Subtract your EFC from the cost of each college to determine your Need for each one.

Regardless of the cause, a request for more information stalls your application until you provide it. Then when you resubmit the form with the overlooked signature or Dad's assets, it will be another four weeks before you learn your magic number, and before your information gets to the colleges of your choice.

If your response is No. 2, an Expected Family Contribution, congratulations! You can now subtract that EFC from the cost of the colleges you are considering and learn your officially designated Need—your magic number.

And it's time to learn a new acronym, SAR. It stands for Student Aid Report, the multipage document you get in the mail that reports your EFC in the upper-right corner of page one. The EFC is the most important information it contains but the SAR serves other useful purposes.

Check your SAR for errors and make a copy for your files before sending it to colleges.

The SAR tells you, usually in the middle of page one, if your EFC is low enough to be eligible for a Pell

Grant. If it is, you probably are in line for a generous package of financial aid built upon the Pell. You'll learn the size of your Pell Grant in your award letter from the college.

Most of the SAR merely regurgitates the information you submitted on your FAFSA. But it's your opportunity to correct errors or poor estimates. You can make corrections on the appropriate lines, send back the SAR, and the amended information will go to your colleges.

When you select a college, you must send your SAR to the financial aid office before it can distribute any aid. If you are eligible for a Pell Grant, the SAR will include a Pell payment voucher that must be sent to your college. But be sure to make a copy for your records. When your financial aid arrives, you'll want to be sure the college was using your correct EFC as reported on the SAR.

PREPARE TO BE VERIFIED

What audit means to taxpayers, verification means to financial aid applicants. It means someone wants to see the records that support the numbers on your form.

The government's computers randomly select about one-third of all applications for verification. If you are selected, your SAR will inform you near the bottom of page one.

It also will tell the colleges to which your information has been sent. The college financial aid office will ask to see your tax returns and other records that back up the information on your form. If you refuse, or you can't find the records, you are disqualified for federal aid.

Colleges also can request verification of any aid application. Most will do so if they see numbers that raise questions such as investment assets but no interest income or different answers to the same question on the FAFSA and PROFILE.

Some college personnel routinely request verification by every applicant. They will let you know who they are in their application packets. Others want verification from every enrolled student who gets aid.

Now let's look at how you get the money.

How the Money Comes to You

...its package can affect your life for years

Here's another word you'll be hearing a bit: package. It's the financial aid folks' term for the combination of grants, loans, and jobs they offer you as an inducement to attend their college. It's your financial aid.

Yes, they consider it an inducement. Although financial aid was conceived to help needy students get into college, and federal programs still serve that goal, most colleges that give away their own money use it as a lure to attract students they want on their campuses.

Thus, you'll also hear the term "preferential packaging." That means the more attractive students get the better deal. Your high school report card could have as much influence on your financial aid as your parents' salaries. I'll talk more about that later in the chapter.

THE AWARD LETTER

A letter spelling out details of your financial aid package will arrive a few days—usually not more than two weeks—after you've

59

Expect to hear about aid soon after you've been accepted.

been notified that you've been admitted. The exceptions are students who waited too long to apply for financial aid and whose data aren't processed when the admission decisions are made.

The package, whatever its size, will be only for one year. You must apply for financial aid again every year you are in school.

Your package will include aid in some, perhaps all, of four categories:

- **Grants.** These can come in one of three forms: need-based grants such as the federal Pell and SEOG, state grants for which you have qualified, or merit-based grants for academics, music, athletics, or other talent. Most grants are outright gifts with no strings. Some impose conditions, such as a minimum grade point average, to be renewed each year.
- **Jobs.** A Work-Study job, which is pay-as-you-go aid, with 75 percent of your wages paid by the federal government. It could be on campus or in the adjacent community. Some schools try to match students with jobs in their field of study.
- **Discounts.** The college may offer you a discount from its published tuition as a form of financial aid. It probably won't be described as a discount in your award letter. It will be described as a grant from the college, although no money will change hands.
- **Loans.** If your Need isn't met from the first three sources, many schools will offer you the opportunity to borrow money at low rates, perhaps with the interest paid by the government while you're in school.

If you are accepted to more than one college, you'll get an award letter from each. Since their packages probably won't be identical, you'll have to consider the aid award along with all the other factors in deciding which offer to accept. If each school offers the same total aid, check the balance of grants vs. loans in each. More grants, of course, is preferable.

The award letter will explain how to get the aid that's not distributed by the school. If it offers you an unsubsidized loan, for example, it could include the standard application form, or suggest you pick one up at your bank.

> **When comparing packages, grants are more valuable than loans.**

You will be asked to sign the award letter, indicating your acceptance of the package, and return it by a certain date or the award will be rescinded and the money given to someone else. But before you sign on the dotted line you will need to check all of the numbers carefully.

CHECK THE NUMBERS

Check the Expected Family Contribution in your award letter to see if it agrees with the EFC calculated from your application. If it doesn't match the EFC on your Student Aid Report (SAR) or the EFC on your FAF acknowledgment notice, call the college financial aid office to ask why.

It could be that you submitted more information directly to the college that adjusted your EFC, or that the college is using its own formula. It could also be human error in the financial aid office, which it should be happy to correct.

Check also the Cost of Attendance used to determine your Need. (Remember the formula: Cost of Attendance − Expected Family Contribution = Need.) Does the Cost of Attendance in your award letter include the cost of transportation, books, and personal miscellaneous expenses, as federal law requires? In other words, is it higher than the published tuition, room and board rates, if you will be a residential student, or higher than tuition if you'll be commut-

If your COA is not higher than the school's published billable costs, call the financial aid office quickly for an adjustment.

ing? If the Cost of Attendance in your award letter isn't higher than those published numbers, the college either has erred or is juggling numbers. And you have a legitimate complaint.

"Most parents don't understand that Cost of Attendance is different than billable cost," says Wendy Beckemeyer, director of admissions and financial aid at Missouri's Cottey College. "They just want to know what they have to pay the school."

But when you call, for whatever reason, be patient. Scores of your peers who just got award letters are also calling with questions. The days after award letters go out are notorious for busy signals on financial aid office phones.

SHOULD YOU BORROW?

Now comes a decision that will affect your life for years after you earn a degree. Should you apply for those low-interest loans you are offered?

Consider your options:

- Can you decline the loans and keep the rest of the aid package? Most colleges permit it but some offer the package as all-or-nothing. If your award letter doesn't tell you, ask.
- If you decline the loans, can you find the money elsewhere to attend this college?
- If you decline the loans and can't afford this college, are you prepared to attend a less-expensive school at which you won't have to borrow? Perhaps a community college?

Borrowing for college can be seen, from its downside or its upside, as a curse or a blessing.

From the downside, it ties up a portion of your income in loan repayments for as long as 10 years.

From the upside, it allows you to attend the college that fits you best at a cost of about $200 a month after leaving school. That's an average repayment (based on a total debt of $16,000) but it's probably less than your rent and about the same as your car payment. (See the table below for typical college loan repayment schedules.)

Throughout this book, I mention home and car payments in the same sentences with college loans because those are the three major debts most people accrue. With a college loan, you are paying lower interest for (unless real estate prices suddenly soar) a greater return on an investment than for either a car or house.

The best advice from this author's perspective is to find the college that best suits you—in size, location, type of student body, academic offering, and other nonfinancial factors. Compare costs, then find the money to pay for the college of your choice even if it means a large debt. In the long run, you will have invested wisely.

> **Choose the right school, then find a way to pay for it.**

HOW MUCH YOU REPAY

Here's a typical repayment schedule, starting after the student leaves college, for the Subsidized Stafford Loan, the most popular form of college borrowing. It's based on 8.25 percent interest, the highest rate that can be charged (your interest rate could be lower):

Total borrowed	Number of Payments	Monthly Payment	Interest Charges	Total Repaid
$2,600	65	$ 50.00	$ 628.42	$ 3,228.42
$4,000	120	$ 49.06	$1,887.20	$ 5,887.20
$7,500	120	$ 91.99	$3,538.80	$11,038.80
$10,000	120	$122.65	$4,718.00	$14,718.00
$15,000	120	$188.98	$7,077.60	$22,077.60

Source: U.S. Department of Education

IF YOUR NEED ISN'T MET

If your Need—your magic number—is $9,000 and your aid package totals $6,000, you have been "gapped." That's jargon that means your aid falls short of your need.

Many colleges can't meet all students' Need simply because they don't have the money. A large number of state colleges, with no cash of their own to give away or prohibited by state laws from offering discounts, spread their government aid to as many students as they can until it runs out. But they often can't meet a student's full Need.

Even colleges that claim they meet all students' Need—that no students are gapped—can define that Need in many ways. They can use the Expected Family Contribution from the FAFSA formula, the EFC from the PROFILE formula, or their own modified EFC.

At colleges offering their own money, aid directors have a budget they can't exceed without falling on bended knee to the college president. They distribute that aid—in discounts off the sticker price—to meet their institution's priorities, encouraging certain students to enroll with generosity, discouraging others with "gaps."

Even at very selective colleges, the admission office may admit three times as many students as it needs for its freshman class

LOAN CANCELLATION

Loans in any of the government's financial aid programs — Perkins, Stafford, or PLUS — are forgiven on the death or total disability of the borrower. Perkins Loans also can be cancelled for the following reasons:

Condition	Cancellation
Full-time teacher in designated school serving low-income students	**Up to 100%**
Full-time special education teacher in public or other nonprofit school	**Up to 100%**
Full-time professional provider of early intervention services for disabled kids	**Up to 100%**
Full-time teacher of math, science, foreign language, or other fields designated as shortage areas	**Up to 100%**
Full-time employee of agency providing services to high-risk or low-income kids	**Up to 100%**
Full-time nurse or medical technician	**Up to 100%**
Full-time law enforcement or corrections officer	**Up to 100%**
Full-time staff member in Head Start program	**Up to 100%**
Service in Peace Corps or VISTA	**Up to 70%**
Services in armed forces in areas of hostilities or imminent danger	**Up to 50%**

Source: U.S. Department of Education

STAFFORD LOAN CEILINGS

These are the maximums that can be borrowed each year by any student under the Stafford Loan program. The total of subsidized and unsubsidized Stafford Loans must be within the ceilings.

Dependent Undergraduate

Freshman:	$2,625
Sophomore:	$3,500
Junior/Senior:	$5,500

Independent Undergraduate

Freshman:	$6,625	(at least $4,000 of this unsubsidized)
Sophomore:	$7,500	(at least $4,000 unsubsidized)
Junior/Senior:	$10,500	(at least $5,000 unsubsidized)
Graduate Student	$18,500	(at least $10,000 unsubsidized)

Source: U.S. Department of Education

because history shows only one third of those accepted will enroll. The financial aid office then uses its resources to attract the most desirable one third.

Colleges that have the money to meet every student's Need and leave no gaps can adjust the aid packages to reflect their priorities. The better students get a higher percentage of grants and discounts; others are offered more loans. That's preferential packaging.

Gettysburg's Shunk puts it very bluntly: "The best grant-to-loan packages go to the students who have the best credentials."

The better students get a higher percentage of grants and discounts; others are offered more loans.

Wendy Beckemeyer at Cottey College says: "I don't think [preferential packaging] is fair from the student's point of view. But from the institution's point of view, when more students are leveraging institutions against each other with bidding wars, it's probably necessary."

If your award letter from a college that offers institutional aid shows a gap between your magic number and Cost of Attendance, it is sending the message: "Sorry, you are not a high priority. If you want to come here, you better find the cash somewhere else."

But remember the difference. Schools that don't give away their own money, like almost all smaller state colleges, award all aid strictly on need. If a gap exists, it's because the government money is gone. At schools that offer discounts, usually private colleges, a gap indicates priorities in student selection.

SETTING THE PRIORITIES

How can you become a high-priority student receiving the most generous financial aid package? Sometimes it's luck. Sometimes it's the result of good planning. Most often, it's because you were a good high school student who the college feels would be a welcome addition to its campus.

If the band director is desperate for a tuba player, and you are adept at the tuba, you are a high priority. That's luck. In other years, and at other schools, tubas won't be in demand.

Of course, your astute high school band director could have been aware of the impending tuba need at a nearby college and pointed you in that direction. You may even have sent a tape of your tuba performances to the college music department at the time you applied. The impressed college band director could have passed the word to the admission office that you have the tuba he desires. You've become a high-priority applicant, a status reflected in your financial aid package. That's good planning.

Tales abound of college faculty departments—physics, economics, whatever—exerting pressure on an admission office to bring them more students. In those years, at those schools, applicants planning to major in physics, economics, or whatever suddenly get a higher priority.

At Florida's Rollins College, Dean David Erdmann reports similar faculty pressure to increase freshman SAT scores. That made test results a top priority.

At the vast majority of colleges, however, the highest priorities go to students who couple excellent academic records with examples of leadership and special talent. That's neither luck nor planning. It's hard work.

AND IF YOU DON'T LIKE YOUR PACKAGE

If you think you're entitled to more financial aid than you are awarded, you can appeal. But the appeal will be heard by the same financial aid director who assembled your package. And from her there is no higher appeal.

Will an appeal succeed? Turn the page, and let's see.

CHAPTER SIX

HOW TO GET MORE

...a little extra work can have profitable results

Let's assume that, just because you're you, you will get some financial aid. Your family's financial situation gives you a magic number that qualifies for a package of grants and loans from the college of your choice.

By doing nothing except filling out and mailing some forms, you will get a few thousand dollars to pay for college. But with a little extra work, you could get more.

That profitable extra work falls into three categories:

- Making yourself more attractive to the college of your choice.
- Persuading the college to raise your magic number
- Finding money the college doesn't control.

KNOW THE AID PEOPLE

It never hurts to have a friend. And a friend in a financial aid office can be valuable indeed.

When you call about that award letter, or with a question about any part of the process, won't you be more comfortable if you know the person on other end of the line? And if you know that person knows you?

Most students ignore the college financial aid office until they get an award letter. Then after one phone call expressing chagrin that the package isn't larger, they forget about it and move on to more interesting pursuits. That attitude, unfortunately, can cost money.

On your initial visit to check out a school, you undoubtedly drop into the admission office, check out the dorms, cafeteria, library, perhaps even the academic department where you intend to major. The financial aid office should be on your list too.

> **You should start getting to know, and be known by, the financial aid folks on your first campus visit.**

Call ahead for an appointment. Explain that you'll be visiting the campus and would like to talk about the aid process. Many financial aid counselors will be happy to chat with you. The visit serves two purposes: you get questions answered in person and you start to build a rapport with someone who will be handling your financial future.

You can ask about the forms required, the school's deadlines, the possibility of merit-based aid. (A list of suggested questions is on page 70.) If your parents are divorced, you should ask how the college will look at your absent parent's finances. And ask if any outside scholarships you earn will be deducted from your financial aid. Some colleges do, some don't.

More importantly, you will begin to present yourself to the financial aid office—as at the admission office—as a student they would like to have. Be friendly, cooperative, and eager to gain information but not pushy. If you don't understand something, ask for an explanation in simple terms.

QUESTIONS FOR THE FINANCIAL AID OFFICE

—How many forms are required? Does the college want its own form in addition to the FAFSA (and possibly the FAF)?

—Does the college have a deadline for processing financial aid requests?

—What kind of high school record qualifies for a "good student" aid package?

—Does the college go strictly by the federal formula for determining need or does it use its own formula for its own money?

—Are out-of-state students more or less likely to qualify than in-staters?

—Does the college offer its own money first, then loans and jobs? Or does it give "self-help" aid first, then fill in with grants?

—Can parts of a financial aid package be declined while other parts are accepted?

When you get home, send a thank-you note to the counselor. Tell her how much you appreciate her advice and what a big help she has been. Financial aid folks are among the most isolated on campus. They value the few kind words they receive.

Send a thank-you note; then keep in touch.

When you mail your FAFSA, call or drop a line to the counselor reminding her of your visit and informing her you have applied for financial aid. Ask her to call you if she has questions. You could be the only student all year to offer such an invitation. She'll like that.

When the time comes to assemble an award package, you will be an individual—not just a collection of paper or numbers on a screen. If priorities for aid are being set, it can't hurt, and it could very well help.

"Students are intimidated by financial aid," says Brenda Smith, aid director at Cottey College. "Their parents have handled the financial side of their lives, and still do. It would be beneficial for the student to develop a personal relationship with the financial aid office."

PROFESSIONAL JUDGMENT

File those two words, "professional judgment," near the front of your memory. They are from the federal law regulating financial aid.

What they mean is: "Nothing in this law is carved in stone. Anything can be adjusted by the professional judgment of the college financial aid director."

Every financial aid director in the country can use his professional judgment to raise or lower your magic number, offer you aid without regard to your magic number, or throw out the data on your FAFSA and build a new magic number from scratch. However, circumstances must be pretty persuasive for any of these to happen.

Throwing out the FAFSA and starting over occurred extensively at Midwest colleges after the 1993 floods. Parents whose businesses were wiped out were allowed to estimate their current year's income to replace earnings reported for the previous year. And their kids' magic numbers soared.

To alter a student's award through professional judgment, a financial aid director must have a sound reason. And she isn't going to be out looking for it. You must bring the good reason to her.

Give the financial aid director a good reason to increase your award, if you can.

If anything has changed financially for you or your family since you filed your forms, it could change your aid eligibility. Changes in personal situations—a serious illness, a divorce, severe damage to a home—also could affect your aid status.

Call or write the financial aid office to report such a change. Ask for an interview to explain it. (If you know someone in the office by this time, you will be more comfortable making the request.) The aid director could decide that, in his professional judgment, you are entitled to more money.

But be persuasive. From professional judgment, there is no appeal.

A BIDDING WAR?

A father who called USA TODAY's Financial Aid Hot Line in 1993 compared shopping for college to buying a car. In his analogy, financial aid directors are the car salesmen, each ready to beat the competition by $100 to close the deal.

Yes, they are out there. The kind of financial aid director who'll tell a parent: "Bring your best offer to me, and I'll top it. I guarantee your kid will get a better deal at Old Siwash than any place on the East Coast."

That aid director is under pressure from his president, his faculty or both to bring in a certain type of student. In the jargon of his colleagues, he's buying a freshman class. And he represents a small minority of the nation's aid directors.

By informing College A that College B has made a better offer, you can't lose—and you might just gain.

While outright bidding wars for students occur rarely, negotiation certainly is possible. If your aid package from the college of your choice is, say, $500 to $1,000 lower than from a less desirable school, call or write the aid office before the deadline on the award letter.

Explain that Ivy U. is your first choice but, because Old Siwash is offering more aid, you probably will be forced to enroll there. The Ivy U. aid director might say she'll take another look at your file to see what she could have missed. In a day or two, she might call back matching Old Siwash.

FINDING OTHER MONEY

The folks at Princeton like to talk about Meta Jones, a student from a Washington, D.C., ghetto who paid her $22,000 bill in 1991 with no financial aid, using none of her or her parents' money. She raised it all in private scholarships.

Meta was a hustler. She beat the bushes. She spent hours in libraries poring over lists of foundations that give grants to good students. She bugged her guidance office for notices of clubs and churches offering scholarships. She wrote to the foundations, clubs and churches asking their criteria for giving away money, then convinced them that she qualified. She raised more than $29,000.

"I wanted to be in a position to choose among the colleges that accepted me based on where I wanted to go, not where I could afford to go," says Jones. "The money is out there, but many students don't find the channels to get it."

Every high school student does not have the energy, or the outstanding academic record, of Meta Jones. But a small fraction of $29,000 would help. And it's there often just for the asking.

Thousands of scholarships are offered each year apart from the college financial aid process.

Some scholarships are awarded just for academic excellence. Others have stipulations, going to students of certain religions or ethnic origins, children of veterans, students who intend to specialize in certain fields, members of organizations or labor unions, children of company employees. And there are many with narrower restrictions.

Pennsylvania's Lafayette College has a scholarship, never used, limited to residents of West Palm Beach, Fla. Other schools have scholarships for students with certain surnames. Amherst College has a grant for a student who can't get any other scholarships. Such offbeat grants usually come from philanthropic bequests.

If you qualify for an offbeat scholarship, like one limited to red-haired daughters of dairy farmers, your financial aid office eagerly will tell you. They're difficult to give away.

But for most of the grants you, like Meta, are on your own. The best place to start your search is with computer programs. Two software programs, one produced by Peterson's and the other by The College Board and sold to schools

Start your scholarship search with a computer program.

and libraries, offer comprehensive national lists. They ask you to enter a full personal profile, then tell you what's out there that you might qualify for and how to find it.

Each high school guidance office should have one of the scholarship programs on a PC. If your's doesn't, start calling public and college libraries until you find one that does. Several directories available at most libraries offer similar information in book form.

From the computer, you'll get a printout listing names, addresses, and phone numbers of organizations offering scholarships for which you could qualify. The amount of money the list will make available to you will be directly related to the time you spend requesting information from the scholarship organizations, studying their criteria, and applying for their grants.

Meta Jones says she applied for 55 grants during her high school senior year and got seven. But seven was enough.

"Make a list of everything you've done," she advises, "then look for someone who might be giving money for that activity. If you spent one day working in a diabetes center, someone in that health care field might be offering a scholarship."

SHOULD YOU PAY SOMEONE TO SEARCH FOR YOU?

That's up to you. There are many services that will take your money to hunt scholarships for you. But what you get for your cash usually is what you could find for yourself from a computer: a list of organizations for whose grants you could qualify. You're still on your own to apply, and to persuade those groups that you deserve their money.

"I've heard too many stories of people spending money on a search service and not getting much out of it," says Smith at

"Search services need to be used with care."

Cottey College. "Most of it you can find yourself if you're willing to invest the time."

The National Association of Student Financial Aid Administrators, in a guidebook for high school counselors, cautions: "Search services need to be used with care after a thorough investigation of the services they render. The value of the information provided varies widely."

CHAPTER SEVEN

HOW OTHERS DO IT

...a stroll through the process with three students

Meet Jennifer, Michael, and Melissa. They are typical high school seniors. Each of them has strong academic credentials good enough to get into some selective colleges and, indeed, have been accepted to five. But each has a very different background and financial situation. Their need for money to pay for college varies—so will their fates at the financial aid offices when they apply.

Jennifer Oneder, Michael Twofer, and Melissa Threeby are not real. They are hypothetical students created for this book. The colleges to which they have applied, however, are very real. To help us describe the process in human terms, financial aid directors at five colleges agreed to consider applications from the fictitious students and award aid packages just as they would to any other applicant.

Three of the five are private colleges: the University of Notre Dame in Indiana, Gettysburg College in Pennsylvania, and Cottey College in Missouri. The other two are among the more selective state institutions: the University of North Carolina–Chapel Hill and the College of William & Mary in Williamsburg, Virginia.

Jennifer, Michael, and Melissa each diligently filled out the FAFSA and PROFILE, reproduced in this chapter. The financial circumstances they report, for themselves and their parents, determine their EFC, their magic number, and the aid packages they will get. After we see how each student fares, we can change their particular circumstances to see what could have happened had things been a little different in their lives.

We can also move their residences so each can be considered an in-state and out-of-state student at the two public colleges. Like most state-supported institutions, costs for out-of-staters (and thus financial need) are roughly double the price for home folks. And because Cottey College is all female, for that application we will change Michael to Michelle.

But even their original applications produce aid packages that differ widely from school to school. Jennifer gets $14,125 at Gettysburg, merely $1,910 at Cottey. Michael is awarded $18,675 at Gettysburg, $8,775 at Notre Dame. Melissa, the most affluent of the three, strikes out at four colleges but gets $6,375 from Notre Dame. Let's look at them one by one.

JENNIFER ONEDER

Jennifer lives in Firstville, Virginia, and is the daughter of Oscar and Olivia Oneder (pronounced Won-der). Her father, after graduation from college, got a job teaching math at Firstville High and has been there since. Her mother works part time as a travel agent. Dad is 46, Mom 45. Brother Jason, 20, commutes to Firstville State College.

Last year Oscar earned $35,341 in salary and Olivia picked up $3,747 in travel commissions. But Oscar, even on a teacher's pay, is a diligent saver. For 20 years, he has been putting money regularly into mutual funds. It has grown to a nest egg of almost $125,000. Last year it produced dividends and capital gains of $9,657.

Jennifer, working after school, weekends, and in the summer as a sales clerk in a bookstore, made almost twice as much as Mom—

$6,762. For every birthday since she was born, Jennifer's grandmother gives her $200 to put away for college. She puts it in a bank where it's now worth $4,600.

The Oneders bought a new home in 1987 for $91,000. They caught the last years of the real estate boom and its value has appreciated to $125,000. Their mortgage balance is $68,000, giving them a home equity of $57,000.

All of the above is reported in the proper places on Jennifer's FAFSA and PROFILE. And when it's pushed through the formula, it produces:

JENNIFER'S MAGIC NUMBER

Let's take the numbers from the FAFSA, put them on the worksheet from Chapter Two, referring as needed to the tables also in Chapter Two, and see what comes out.

Jennifer's parents last year had a total income of $48,835. That's easy. They paid $5,044 in federal taxes, taken right off their return. Their allowance for other taxes, as Virginia residents (from Table 1), is 7 percent of their income—$3,418. They paid $2,997 in Social Security tax (FICA). All of these numbers go on the worksheet under Allowances.

Checking Table 4, you see a family of four with two members in college is allowed to protect $14,810 of its income. That's listed as an Allowance. And the Allowance for working parents is 35 percent of Mom's meager earnings, or $1,311.

Add them up on your calculator and you get the Oneder Parents' total Allowances of $27,580. Subtract that from their income and you have $21,255—income the formula considers "available" to pay for college.

For assets, the Oneders have $1,650 in a checking account and $124,381 in mutual funds. That's a net worth, as FAFSA defines it,

(Continued on page 87)

Free Application for Federal Student Aid

WARNING: If you purposely give false or misleading information on
this form, you may be fined $10,000, sent to prison, or both.

"You" and "your" on this form always mean the student who wants aid.

FFFFF

Form Approved
OMB No. 1840-0110
APP. EXP. 6/30/97

U.S. Department of Education
Student Financial
Assistance Programs

Section A: Yourself

1–3. Your name

1. Last: O NE D E R
2. First: J E N N I F E R
3. M.I.

Your title (optional)   Mr. ☐ 1   Miss, Ms., or Mrs. ☐ 2

4–7. Your permanent mailing address
*(All mail will be sent to this
address. See Instructions, page 2
for state/country abbreviations.)*

4. Number and street (Include apt. no.): 1 1 1 1 FI R S T S T
5. City: FIRSTVILLE
6. State: V A
7. ZIP code: 1 1 1 1 1

8. Your permanent home
telephone number

Area code: 8 0 4   5 5 5   1 2 1 2

9. Your state of legal residence

State: V A

10. Date you became a legal resident of the state in question 9
(See Instructions, page 2.)

Month 1 1   Day 2 6   Year 7 6

11–12. Your driver's license number *(Include the state abbreviation. If
you don't have a license, leave this question blank.)*

State: ☐

13. Your social security number
(Don't leave blank. See Instructions, page 3.)

1 1 1 1 1 1 1 1 1

14. Your date of birth

Month 1 1   Day 2 6   Year 7 6

15–16. Are you a U.S. citizen? *(See Instructions, page 3.)*

Yes, I am a U.S. citizen. ☒ 1

No, but I am an eligible noncitizen. ☐ 2

A

No, neither of the above. ☐ 3

17. As of **today**, are you married? *(Check only one box.)*

I am not married. (I am single,
widowed, or divorced.) ☐ 1

I am married. ☐ 2

I am separated from my spouse. ☐ 3

18. Date you were married, widowed, separated,
or divorced. If divorced, use earliest
date of divorce or separation.

Month ☐ ☐   Year ☐ ☐

19. Will you have your first bachelor's
degree before July 1, 1996?   Yes ☐ 1   No ☐ 2

Section B: Your Plans

20. Your year in college during the 1996–97 school year
(Check only one box.)

1st ☒ 1   3rd ☐ 3   5th year or more undergraduate ☐ 5

2nd ☐ 2   4th ☐ 4   graduate ☐ 6

21–24. Your expected enrollment status for the 1996–97 school year
(See Instructions, page 3.)

School term	Full time	3/4 time	1/2 time	Less than 1/2 time	Not enrolled
21. Summer term '96	☐ 1	☐ 2	☐ 3	☐ 4	☒ 5
22. Fall sem./quarter '96	☒ 1	☐ 2	☐ 3	☐ 4	☐ 5
23. Winter quarter '96–'97	☒ 1	☐ 2	☐ 3	☐ 4	☐ 5
24. Spring sem./quarter '97	☒ 1	☐ 2	☐ 3	☐ 4	☐ 5

25–26. Your degree/certificate
and course of study
(See Instructions, page 3.)

25. Degree/certificate ☐

26. Course of study: 0 7

27. Date you expect to complete
your degree/certificate

Month 0 6   Day   Year 0 0

28–30. In addition to grants, what other types of financial
aid are you (and your parents) interested in?
(Check one or more boxes.)

• Work-study ☒ 1

• Student loans ☒ 2

• Parent loans for students (Federal PLUS) ☒ 3

31. If you are (or were) in college, do you plan
to attend that same college in 1996–97?

Yes ☐ 1   No ☐ 2

32. For how many dependent children will you
pay child care expenses in 1996–97? ☐

33–34. Veterans education benefits you expect to
receive from July 1, 1996, through June 30, 1997

33. Amount per month $_____ .00

34. Number of months ☐ ☐

Section C: Education Background

Page 2

35–36. Date that you (the student) received, or will receive, your high school diploma, either—

- by graduating from high school
  | 0 | 6 | 9 | 6 |
  Month   Year

  OR

- by earning a GED
  | | | | | |
  Month   Year

(Enter one date. Leave blank if the question does not apply to you.)

37–38. Highest grade level completed by your father and your mother *(Check one box for each parent. See Instructions, page 4.)*

	37. Father	38. Mother
elementary school (K–8)	☐1	☐1
high school (9–12)	☐2	☒2
college or beyond	☒3	☐3
unknown	☐4	☐4

Section D: Federal Family Education Loan (FFEL) Program Information

(Leave this section blank if you have never received a Federal Stafford Loan, a guaranteed student loan [GSL], or a Federal Insured Student Loan [FISL].)

39. If you borrowed under the Federal Stafford, Federal SLS, Federal PLUS, or Federal Consolidation Loan program and there is an outstanding balance on your loan(s), enter the date of your oldest outstanding loan.

| | | | | |
Month   Year

40–41. Write in the total outstanding balance(s) on your Federal Stafford and Federal SLS Loans.

Amount owed

40. Federal Stafford Loan(s) $_____.00

41. Federal SLS Loan(s) $_____.00

42. Check one box to indicate the interest rate you have on your outstanding Federal Stafford Loan.

7% ☐1   9% ☐3   Variable ☐5

8% ☐2   8%/10% ☐4

43–44. Do you currently have a Federal PLUS Loan or a Consolidation Loan?

	Yes	No
43. Federal PLUS Loan	☐1	☐2
44. Federal Consolidation Loan	☐1	☐2

Section E: Student Status

	Yes	No
45. Were you born **before** January 1, 1973?	☐1	☒2
46. Are you a veteran of the U.S. Armed Forces?	☐1	☒2
47. Will you be a graduate or professional student in 1996–97?	☐1	☒2
48. Are you married?	☐1	☒2
49. Are you a ward of the court or are both your parents dead?	☐1	☒2
50. Do you have legal dependents *(other than a spouse)* that fit the definition in Instructions, page 4?	☐1	☒2

If you answered **"Yes"** to **any** question in Section E, go to Section F and fill out the **GRAY** and the **WHITE** areas on the rest of the form.

If you answered **"No"** to **every** question in Section E, go to Section F, and fill out the **BLUE** and the **WHITE** areas on the rest of the form.

Section F: Household Information

If you are filling out the GRAY and WHITE areas, answer questions 51 and 52, and go to Section G.

If you are filling out the BLUE and WHITE areas, skip questions 51 and 52. Answer questions 53 through 57 about your parents, and then go on to Section G.

STUDENT (& SPOUSE)

51. Number of family members in 1996–97 (Include yourself and your spouse. Include your children and other people only if they meet the definition in Instructions, page 5.) | |

52. Number of college students in 1996–97 (Of the number in 51, how many will be in college at least half-time for at least one term? Include yourself. *See Instructions, page 5.*) | |

PARENTS

53. Your parents' current marital status:

single ☐1   separated ☐3   widowed ☐5

married ☐2   divorced ☐4

54. Your parents' state of legal residence | V | A |

55. Date your parent(s) became legal resident(s) of the state in question 54 *(See Instructions, page 5.)*
| 0 | 8 | | | | 7 | 0 |
Month   Day   Year

56. Number of family members in 1996–97 (Include yourself and your parents. Include your parents' other children and other people only if they meet the definition in Instructions, page 5.) | 0 | 4 |

57. Number of college students in 1996–97 (Of the number in 56, how many will be in college at least half-time for at least one term? Include yourself. *See Instructions, page 6.*) | 2 |

Section G: 1995 Income, Earnings, and Benefits

Everyone must fill out the Student (& Spouse) column. *Page 3*

*(You **must** see the instructions for income and taxes that you should exclude from questions in this section.)*

STUDENT (& SPOUSE)	PARENTS

58. The following 1995 U.S. income tax figures are from: *(Check only one box.)*

a completed 1995 IRS Form 1040A or 1040EZ	(Go to 59)	[X] ₁
a completed 1995 IRS Form 1040	(Go to 59)	☐ ₂
an estimated 1995 IRS Form 1040A or 1040EZ	(Go to 59)	☐ ₃
an estimated 1995 IRS Form 1040	(Go to 59)	☐ ₄
A U.S. income tax return will not be filed.	(Skip to 62)	☐ ₅

69. The following 1995 U.S. income tax figures are from: *(Check only one box.)*

a completed 1995 IRS Form 1040A or 1040EZ	(Go to 70)	☐ ₁
a completed 1995 IRS Form 1040	(Go to 70)	[X] ₂
an estimated 1995 IRS Form 1040A or 1040EZ	(Go to 70)	☐ ₃
an estimated 1995 IRS Form 1040	(Go to 70)	☐ ₄
A U.S. income tax return will not be filed.	(Skip to 73)	☐ ₅

1995 total number of exemptions (Form 1040-line 6e, or 1040A-line 6e; 1040EZ filers—*see Instructions, pages 6 & 7.*) **59.** | 0 0 |

70. | 0 ₁ 4 |

1995 Adjusted Gross Income (AGI-Form 1040-line 31, 1040A-line 16, or 1040EZ-line 4, or *see Instructions, pages 6 & 7.*) **60.** $ 6,762 .00 — **TAX FILERS ONLY** — **71.** $ 48,835 .00

1995 U.S. income tax paid (Form 1040-line 46, 1040A-line 25, or 1040EZ-line 8) **61.** $ 476 .00

72. $ 5,044 .00

1995 Income earned from work   Student **62.** $ 6,746 .00   Father **73.** $ 35,431 .00

1995 Income earned from work   Spouse **63.** $ .00   Mother **74.** $ 3,747 .00

1995 Untaxed income and benefits (yearly totals only)

Social security benefits **64.** $ .00   **75.** $ .00

Aid to Families with Dependent Children (AFDC or ADC) **65.** $ .00   **76.** $ .00

Child support received for all children **66.** $ .00   **77.** $ .00

Other untaxed income and benefits from Worksheet #2, page 11 **67.** $ .00   **78.** $ .00

1995 Title IV Income Exclusions from Worksheet #3, page 12 **68.** $ .00   **79.** $ .00

Section H: Information Release

80-91. What college(s) do you plan to attend in 1996–97?
(Note: By answering this question, you are giving permission to send your application data to the college(s) you list below.)

Housing codes	1 = on-campus	3 = with parent(s)
	2 = off-campus	4 = with relative(s) other than parent(s)

	College name	Address (or code, see Instructions, page 7)	City	State	Housing codes
80.					81.
82.					83.
84.					85.
86.					87.
88.					89.
90.					91.

92. Do you give the U.S. Department of Education permission to send information from this form to the financial aid agencies in your state as well as to the state agencies of all of the colleges listed above?   Yes ☐ ₁ No ☐ ₂

(States and colleges may require additional information and may have their own deadlines for applying for financial aid. Be sure to see "Deadlines for State Student Aid" in Instructions, page 10.)

93. Check this box if you give Selective Service permission to register you. *(See Instructions, page 8.)*   ☐ ₁

94–95. Read and Sign   *Page 4*

Certification: All of the information provided by me or any other person on this form and in Section I, if completed, is true and complete to the best of my knowledge. I understand that this application is being filed jointly by all signatories. If asked by an authorized official, I agree to give proof of the information that I have given on this form and in Section I, if completed. I realize that this proof may include a copy of my U.S., state, or local income tax return. I also realize that if I do not give proof when asked, the student may be denied aid.

School Use Only

Dependency override: enter I

Title IV Inst. Number

FAA signature: |

94. Everyone giving information on this form must sign below. If you do not sign this form, it will be returned unprocessed.

MDE Use Only Spec.   No.
(Do not write in this box.) handle   copies

1 Student

If you (and your family) have unusual circumstances, such as:

2 Student's spouse

- tuition expenses at an elementary or secondary school,
- unusual medical or dental expenses, not covered by insurance,
- a family member who is a dislocated worker, or
- other unusual circumstances that might affect your eligibility for student financial aid, you should—
    Check with the financial aid office at your college.

3 Father/Stepfather

4 Mother/Stepmother

95. Date completed **0 1** **0 7** Year **1996** [x]
      Month Day   **1997** [ ]

Preparer's Use Only *(For preparers other than student and parents. Student and parents, sign above. See Instructions, page 8.)*

Preparer's name

96. Employer identification number (EIN)

Last   First   M.I.

97. Preparer's social security number

Firm's name and address (or preparer's, if self-employed)

Certification:
All of the information on this form and in Section I, if completed, is true and complete to the best of my knowledge.

Firm name

Number and street (Include apt. no.)

City   State   ZIP code

98. Preparer's signature   **Date**

———— ATTENTION ————

If you are filling out the GRAY and WHITE areas, go to Instructions, page 8, and complete **WORKSHEET A. This will tell you whether you must fill out Section I.** If you meet certain tax filing and income conditions, you may skip Section I.

If you are filling out the BLUE and WHITE areas, go to Instructions, page 8, and complete **WORKSHEET B. This will tell you whether you must fill out Section I.** If you meet certain tax filing and income conditions, you may skip Section I.

Section I: Asset Information

	STUDENT (& SPOUSE)		PARENTS	
		106. Age of your older parent		**4 6**
Cash, savings, and checking accounts	**99.** $ 450 .00		**107.** $ 1,650 .00	
Other real estate and investments value *(Don't include the home.)*	**100.** $ 4,600 .00		**108.** $ 124,381 .00	
Other real estate and investments debt *(Don't include the home.)*	**101.** $ 0 .00		**109.** $ .00	
Business value	**102.** $ 0 .00		**110.** $ .00	
Business debt	**103.** $ 0 .00		**111.** $ .00	
Farm value *(See Instructions, pages 8 & 9.)*	**104.** $ 0 .00		**112.** $ .00	
Farm debt *(See Instructions, pages 8 & 9.)*	**105.** $ 0 .00		**113.** $ .00	

MAKE SURE THAT YOU HAVE COMPLETED, DATED, AND SIGNED THE APPLICATION.
Mail the application to: Federal Student Aid Programs, P.O. Box 4016, Iowa City, IA 52243-4016.

Jennifer Oneder
CSS No. 1234567
111-11-1111

Financial Aid *P*ROFILE — 1996-97

Complete all sections of the PROFILE Form except Section E. Be certain that everyone giving information on the form signs it.

Section A — Student's Information

1. How many family members will the student (and spouse) support in 1996-97? List their names and give information about them in M. See instructions. | 0 |

2. Of the number in 1, how many will be in college at least half-time for at least one term in 1996-97? Include yourself. | 0, 0 |

3. What is the student's state of legal residence? | V, A |

4. What is the student's citizenship status?
   a. 1 ☒ U.S. citizen
      2 ☐ Permanent resident
      3 ☐ Neither of the above (Answer "b" and "c" below.)
   b. Country of citizenship?
   c. Visa classification?
      1 ☐ F1   2 ☐ F2   3 ☐ J1   4 ☐ J2   5 ☐ Other

Section B — Student's 1995 Income & Benefits

Don't report parents' information on this page. If married, include spouse's information in Sections B, C, D, and E.

5. The following 1995 U.S. Income tax return figures are (Mark only one box.)
   1 ☒ estimated. Will file IRS Form 1040EZ or 1040A. Go to 6.
   2 ☐ estimated. Will file IRS Form 1040. Go to 6.
   3 ☐ from a completed IRS Form 1040EZ or 1040A. Go to 6.
   4 ☐ from a completed IRS Form 1040. Go to 6.
   5 ☐ a tax return will not be filed. Skip to 10.

Tax Filers Only

6. 1995 total number of exemptions (IRS Form 1040, line 6e or 1040A, line 6e or 1040EZ — see instructions) **6.** | 0 |

7. 1995 Adjusted Gross Income from IRS Form 1040, line 31 or 1040A, line 13 or 1040EZ, line 3 (Use the worksheet in the instructions.) **7.** $ 6,762 .00

8. 1995 U.S. income tax paid (IRS Form 1040, line 47 or 1040A, line 22 or 1040EZ, line 9) **8.** $ 476 .00

9. 1995 itemized deductions (IRS Form 1040, Schedule A, line 26. Write in "0" if deductions were not itemized.) **9.** $ 0 .00

10. 1995 income earned from work by student (See instructions.) **10.** $ 6,746 .00

11. 1995 income earned from work by student's spouse **11.** $ 0 .00

12. 1995 dividend and interest income **12.** $ 16 .00

13. 1995 untaxed income and benefits (Give total amount for the year.)
   a. Social security benefits (See instructions.) **13. a.** $ 0 .00
   b. Aid to Families with Dependent Children **b.** $ 0 .00
   c. Child support received for all the student's children **c.** $ 0 .00
   d. Earned Income Credit (IRS Form 1040, line 56 or 1040A, line 28c) **d.** $ 0 .00
   e. Other – write total from worksheet, page X. **e.** $ 0 .00

14. 1995 earnings from Federal Work-Study or other need-based work programs plus any grant and scholarship aid in excess of tuition, fees, books, and supplies **14.** $ 0 .00

Section C — Student's Assets

15. Cash, savings, and checking accounts $ 450 .00

	What is it worth today?	What is owed on it?
16. Investments (Including Uniform Gifts to Minors. See instructions.)	$ 4,600 .00	$ 0 .00
17. Home (Renters write in "0.")	$ 0 .00	$ .00
18. Other real estate	$ 0 .00	$ .00
19. Business and farm	$ 0 .00	$ .00

20. If the farm is included in 19, is the student living on the farm?   Yes ☐ 1   No ☐ 2

21. If student owns home, give
   a. year purchased | 1,9 | | | b. purchase price $ 0 .00

Section D — Student's Trust Information

22. a. Total value of all trust(s) $ 0 .00
   b. Is any income or part of the principal currently available?   Yes ☐ 1   No ☐ 2
   c. Who established the trust(s)?   1 ☐ Student's parents   2 ☐ Other

Section E — Student's Expenses

23. 1995 child support paid by student $ 0 .00

24. 1995 medical and dental expenses not covered by insurance (See instructions.) $ 0 .00

Section F — Student's Expected Summer/School-Year Resources for 1996-97

	Amount per month	Number of months
25. Student's veterans benefits (July 1, 1996 – June 30, 1997)	$ _____ .00	☐☐

26. Student's (and spouse's) resources
(Don't enter monthly amounts.)

	Summer 1996 (3 months)	School Year 1996-97 (9 months)
a. Student's wages, salaries, tips, etc.	$ 2,000 .00	$ 0 .00
b. Spouse's wages, salaries, tips, etc.	$ 0 .00	$ 0 .00
c. Other taxable income	$ 0 .00	$ 0 .00
d. Untaxed income and benefits	$ 0 .00	$ 0 .00
e. Grants, scholarships, fellowships, etc. from other than the colleges to which the student is applying (List sources in Section P.)		$ 0 .00
f. Tuition benefits from the parents' and/or the student's or spouse's employer		$ 0 .00
g. Contributions from the student's parent(s)		$ 0 .00
h. Contributions from other relatives, spouse's parents, and all other sources		$ 0 .00

Section G — Parents' Household Information – See page X of the instruction booklet.

27. How many family members will your parents support in 1996-97? <u>Always include yourself (the student).</u> List their names and give information about them in M. [0,4]

28. Of the number in 27, how many will be in college at least half-time for at least one term in 1996-97? Include the student. [2]

29. How many parents will be in college at least half-time in 1996-97? (Mark only one box.)
1 ☒ Neither parent   2 ☐ One parent   3 ☐ Both parents

30. What is the current marital status of your parents? (Mark only one box.)
1 ☐ single   3 ☐ separated   5 ☐ widowed
2 ☒ married   4 ☐ divorced

31. What is your parents' state of legal residence? [V,A]

Section H — Parents' Expenses

	1995	Expected 1996
32. Child support paid by the parent(s) completing this form	32 a. $ 0 .00	32. b. $ 0 .00
33. Repayment of educational loans (See instructions.)	33 a. $ 0 .00	33. b. $ 0 .00
34. Medical and dental expenses not covered by insurance (See instructions.)	34 a. $ 0 .00	34. b. $ 0 .00
35. Total elementary, junior high school, and high school tuition paid for dependent children		
Amount paid (Don't include tuition paid for the student.)	35 a. $ 0 .00	35c. $ 0 .00
For how many dependent children? (Don't include the student.)	b. ☐☐	d. ☐☐

Section I — Parents' Assets – If parents own all or part of a business or farm, write in its name and the percent of ownership in Section P.

36. Cash, savings, and checking accounts $ 1,650 .00

37. Monthly home mortgage or rental payment (If none, explain in Section P.) $ 981 .00

	What is it worth today?	What is owed on it?
40. Business	$ _____ .00	$ _____ .00
41. a. Farm	$ _____ .00	$ _____ .00

b. Does family live on the farm?
Yes ☐ 1   No ☐ 2

	What is it worth today?	What is owed on it?
38. Investments	$ 124,381 .00	$ _____ .00
39a. Home (Renters write in "0.")	$ 125,000 .00	$ 68,000 .00

b. year purchased [1,9,8,7]   c. purchase price $ 91,000 .00

42. a. Other real estate $ _____ .00 $ _____ .00

b. year purchased [1,9, ,]   c. purchase price $ _____ .00

*P*ROFILE — 1996-97

Section J — Parents' 1994 Income and Benefits

43. 1994 **Adjusted Gross Income** (IRS Form 1040, line 31 or 1040A, line 13 or 1040EZ, line 3) $ 43,641 .00

44. 1994 **U.S. Income tax paid** (IRS Form 1040, line 47, 1040A, line 22 or 1040EZ, line 9) $ 4,588 .00

45. 1994 **itemized deductions** (IRS Form 1040, Schedule A, line 26. Write "0" if deductions were not itemized) $ 0 .00

46. 1994 **untaxed income and benefits** (Include the same types of income & benefits that are listed in 53 a – k.) $ 0 .00

Section K — Parents' 1995 Income & Benefits

47. The following 1995 U.S. income tax return figures are (Mark only one box.)

1 ☐ estimated. Will file IRS Form 1040EZ or 1040A. Go to 48.   2 ☒ estimated. Will file IRS Form 1040. Go to 48.   3 ☐ from a completed IRS Form 1040EZ or 1040A. Go to 48.   4 ☐ from a completed IRS Form 1040. Go to 48.   5 ☐ a tax return will not be filed. Skip to 52.

Tax Filers Only

48. 1995 **total number of exemptions** (IRS Form 1040, line 6e or 1040A, line 6e or 1040EZ)   **48.** |0|4|

49. 1995 **Adjusted Gross Income** (IRS Form 1040, line 31 or 1040A, line 13 or 1040EZ, line 3)   **49.** $ 48,835 .00

Breakdown of income in 49

a. **Wages, salaries, tips** (IRS Form 1040, line 7 or 1040A, line 7 or 1040EZ, line 1)   **49 a.** $ 35,431 .00

b. **Interest income** (IRS Form 1040, line 8a or 1040A, line 8a or 1040EZ, line 2)   **b.** $ 3,637 .00

c. **Dividend income** (IRS Form 1040, line 9 or 1040A, line 9)   **c.** $ 6,020 .00

d. **Net income (or loss) from business, farm, rents, royalties, partnerships, estates, trusts, etc.** (IRS Form 1040, lines 12, 18, and 19) If a loss, enter the amount in (parentheses).   **d.** $ 3,747 .00

e. **Other taxable income such as alimony received, capital gains (or losses), pensions, annuities, etc.** (IRS Form 1040, lines 10, 11, 13-15, 16b, 17b, 20, 21b, and 22 or 1040A, line 10)   **e.** $ 0 .00

f. **Adjustments to income** (IRS Form 1040, line 30 or 1040A, line 12c)   **f.** $ 0 .00

50. 1995 **U.S. income tax paid** (IRS Form 1040, line 47, 1040A, line 22 or 1040EZ, line 9)   **50.** $ 5,044 .00

51. 1995 **itemized deductions** (IRS Form 1040, Schedule A, line 26. Write in "0" if deductions were not itemized.)   **51.** $ 0 .00

52. 1995 **Income earned from work by father**   **52.** $ 35,431 .00

53. 1995 **Income earned from work by mother**   **53.** $ 3,747 .00

54. 1995 **untaxed income and benefits** (Give total amount for the year. Do not give monthly amounts.)

a. **Social security benefits**   **54a.** $ 0 .00

b. **Aid to Families with Dependent Children**   **b.** $ 0 .00

c. **Child support received for all children**   **c.** $ 0 .00

d. **Deductible IRA and/or Keogh payments** (See instructions.)   **d.** $ 0 .00

e. **Payments to tax-deferred pension and savings plans** (See instructions.)   **e.** $ 0 .00

f. **Amounts withheld from wages for dependent care and medical spending accounts**   **f.** $ 0 .00

g. **Earned Income Credit** (IRS Form 1040, line 56 or 1040A, line 28c)   **g.** $ 0 .00

h. **Housing, food and other living allowances** (See instructions.)   **h.** $ 0 .00

i. **Tax-exempt interest income** (IRS Form 1040, line 8b or 1040A, line 8b)   **i.** $ 0 .00

j. **Foreign income exclusion** (IRS Form 2555, line 43)   **j.** $ 0 .00

k. **Other** – write in the total from the worksheet in the instructions, page X.   **k.** $ 0 .00

WRITE ONLY IN THE ANSWER SPACES. DO NOT WRITE ANYWHERE ELSE.

Section L — Parents' 1996 Expected Income & Benefits
(If the expected total income and benefits will differ from the 1995 total income and benefits by $3,000 or more, explain in P.)

55. 1996 **income earned from work by father** $ 37,000 .00   **57.** 1996 **other taxable income** $ 8,000 .00

56. 1996 **income earned from work by mother** $ 4,000 .00   **58.** 1996 **untaxed income and benefits** $ .00

Section M —Family Member Listing — Give information for all family members but don't give information about yourself. List up to seven other family members here. If there are more than seven, list first those who will be in college at least half-time. List the others in Section P.

59.

Full name of family member / You — the student applicant	Age	Claimed as tax exemption in 1995? Yes? No?	Use codes from below.	1995-96 school year Name of school or college	Year in school	Scholarships and grants	Parents' contri- bution	1996-97 school year Attend college at least one term full-time half-time	Name of school or college
1								₁☐ ₂☐	
2 Oscar Oneder	46	☒ ☐	1					₁☐ ₂☐	
3 Olivia Oneder	45	☒ ☐	1					₁☐ ₂☐	
4 Jason Oneder	20	☒ ☐	3	Firstville St.	2	0	4,500	₁☒ ₂☐	Firstville St.
5		☐ ☐						₁☐ ₂☐	
6		☐ ☐						₁☐ ₂☐	
7		☐ ☐						₁☐ ₂☐	
8		☐ ☐						₁☐ ₂☐	

Write in the correct code from the right. ↑   1 = Student's parent   3 = Student's brother or sister   5 = Student's son or daughter   7 = Other
2 = Student's stepparent   4 = Student's husband or wife   6 = Student's grandparent

Section N — Parents' Information

60. Mark one: ☒ Father ☐ Stepfather ☐ Legal guardian ☐ Other (Explain in P.)

a. Name Oscar Oneder   Age 4 6

b. Mark if: ☐ Self-employed ☐ Unemployed – Date last employed: _____

c. Occupation Teacher

d. Employer Firstville School Board   No. years 23

e. Work telephone (optional) |_|_|_|-|_|_|_|-|_|_|_|_|

f. Retirement plans: ☒ Social security ☒ Union/employer ☐ Civil service/state ☐ IRA/Keogh/tax-deferred ☐ Military ☐ Other

61. Mark one: ☒ Mother ☐ Stepmother ☐ Legal guardian ☐ Other (Explain in P.)

a. Name Olivia Oneder   Age 4 5

b. Mark if: ☒ Self-employed ☐ Unemployed – Date last employed: _____

c. Occupation Travel Agent

d. Employer _____ No. years 7

e. Work telephone (optional) |_|_|_|-|_|_|_|-|_|_|_|_|

f. Retirement plans: ☒ Social security only ☐ Union/employer ☐ Civil service/state ☐ IRA/Keogh/tax-deferred ☐ Military ☐ Other

Section O — Divorced, Separated, or Remarried Parents

(To be answered by the parent who completes this form, if the student's natural or adoptive parents are divorced, separated, or remarried.)

62. a. Year of separation |_|_| Year of divorce |_|_|

b. Other parent's name _____

Home address _____

Occupation/Employer _____

c. According to court order, when will support for the student end? |_|_| |_|_| Month   Year

d. Who last claimed the student as a tax exemption? _____ Year? |_|_|

e. How much does the other parent plan to contribute to the student's education for the 1995-96 school year? $ _____.00

f. Is there an agreement specifying this contribution for the student's education? Yes ☐ No ☐

Section P — Explanations/Special Circumstances
Use this space to explain any unusual expenses such as high medical or dental expenses, educational and other debts, child care, elder care, or special circumstances. Also, give information for any outside scholarships you have been awarded.

Certification:

All the information on this form is true and complete to the best of my knowledge. If asked, I agree to give proof of the information that I have given on this form. I realize that this proof may include a copy of my U.S., state, or local income tax returns. I certify that all information is correct at this time, and that I will send timely notice of any significant change in family income or assets, financial situation, college plans of other children, or the receipt of other scholarships or grants.

1 _____ Student's signature

2 _____ Student's spouse's signature

3 _____ Father's (stepfather's) signature

4 _____ Mother's (stepmother's) signature

Date this form was completed:
|_|_| |_|_| Month Day
1 ☐ 1995
2 ☐ 1996
3 ☐ 1997
Year

of $126,031. In Table 6, you learn that Oscar—as the older parent at age 46—can protect $37,200 of his assets. Subtract that from his net worth and you have $88,831.

That's a number the financial aid folks call Discretionary Net Worth (DNW). And federal law says that 12 percent of DNW should be used to pay for college. Push a few calculator buttons and you learn that 12 percent of $88,831 is $10,660.

The formula has decided Oscar and Olivia have $21,255 in available income and $10,060 in available assets to pay college bills. A total of $31,915. But wait! Not even Congress suggests they spend it all. The formula has one more step (Table 7) that says a certain percentage of that total is all the Oneders should reasonably be expected to pay. That percentage comes to $11,093: the Oneders' expected parental contribution.

But wait again! Remember brother Jason, a full-time college student. The parent contribution gets split two ways, half for Jennifer, half for Jason. For Jennifer, her parents are expected to pay half of $11,093, or $5,547.

Now for Jennifer's own contribution on the worksheet:

Her income is $6,762. Her federal taxes were $476. From the tables, we learn she gets a $270 allowance for other taxes, $516 for Social Security. As a dependent student, the first $1,750 of her income also is deducted. Jennifer has Allowances totaling $3,012. Simple subtraction produces an "available" income of $3,750. The rules say half of that, $1,875, must pay for college.

For assets, Jennifer has $450 in checking and $4,600 in her Grandma's Gifts account, a total of $5,050. And 35 percent of that, or $1,768, also must be used.

Add $1,875 from Jennifer's income and $1,768 from her assets. Her expected contribution is $3,643. Add that to the $5,547 expected from her parents and you have her Expected Family Contribution: $9,190.

Jennifer's EFC is $9,190. The difference between it and the cost of college is her Need—her magic number.

MICHAEL TWOFER

Michael lives in Secondtown, Ohio, with his mother and two younger siblings. His parents, Thomas and Tammy Twofer, have been divorced since 1987. Tammy is a registered nurse working at Secondtown Hospital. Thomas, who remarried, is a physician in Secondtown.

Tammy's job last year paid her $27,356. She had an earned income credit of $1,890 on her federal tax return. Thomas's medical practice paid him $83,260, and he had more than $11,000 in dividend and interest income. He's paying $300 a month child support for each of his three kids until they're 18. Michael's eighteenth birthday is in February of his senior year.

Michael works as a part-time cook at the Secondtown Diner where he earned $1,200 last year. He has no other income or assets. Mom rents their home for $535 a month.

You've probably already guessed that Michael's EFC will be lower and his magic number higher than Jennifer's. Let's see how it works.

MICHAEL'S MAGIC NUMBER

In Secondtown, Ohio, nurses aren't paid very well, and doctors earn a comfortable living. That helps Michael on the FAFSA, which requests financial information only from his custodial parent. His father's $83,000 income is ignored.

Tammy Twofer's total income last year was $29,246. She paid $2,284 in federal taxes. As an Ohio resident (Table 1), she gets credit for 7 percent of her income, or $2,047, for other taxes. Her Social Security taxes were $2,093. In a family of four with one college student (Table 4), $16,670 of Tammy's income is protected. And her employment allowance (Table 3) is the maximum $2,500.

Add up Tammy's Allowances and you have $25,594. When this is deducted from her income, it leaves just $3,652 "available" for

(Continued on page 99)

Free Application for Federal Student Aid

WARNING: If you purposely give false or misleading information on this form, you may be fined $10,000, sent to prison, or both.

"You" and "your" on this form always mean the student who wants aid.

FFFFF

Form Approved
OMB No. 1840-0110
APP. EXP. 6/30/97

U.S. Department of Education
Student Financial
Assistance Programs

Section A: Yourself

1–3. Your name

1. Last   T W O F E R

2. First   M I C H A E L

3. M.I.

Your title (optional)   Mr. ☒ 1   Miss, Ms., or Mrs. ☐ 2

4–7. Your permanent mailing address
(All mail will be sent to this address. See Instructions, page 2 for state/country abbreviations.)

4. Number and street (Include apt. no.)   2 2 2   S E C O N D   A V E

5. City   S E C O N D T O W N

6. State   O H

7. ZIP code   2 2 2 2 2

8. Your permanent home telephone number   51 3 5 5 5 1 2 1 2
Area code

9. Your state of legal residence   O H
State

10. Date you became a legal resident of the state in question 9
(See Instructions, page 2.)   0 2 2 7 7 6
Month   Day   Year

11–12. Your driver's license number *(Include the state abbreviation. If you don't have a license, leave this question blank.)*
State

13. Your social security number   2 2 2 2 2 2 2 2 2
(Don't leave blank. See Instructions, page 3.)

14. Your date of birth   0 2 2 7 7 6
Month   Day   Year

15–16. Are you a U.S. citizen? *(See Instructions, page 3.)*

Yes, I am a U.S. citizen.   ☒ 1

No, but I am an eligible noncitizen.   ☐ 2

A

No, neither of the above.   ☐ 3

17. As of **today**, are you married? *(Check only one box.)*

I am not married. (I am single, widowed, or divorced.)   ☒ 1

I am married.   ☐ 2

I am separated from my spouse.   ☐ 3

18. Date you were married, widowed, separated, or divorced. If divorced, use earliest date of divorce or separation.
Month   Year

19. Will you have your first bachelor's degree before July 1, 1996?   Yes ☐ 1   No ☒ 2

Section B: Your Plans

20. Your year in college during the 1996–97 school year
(Check only one box.)

1st ☒ 1   3rd ☐ 3   5th year or more undergraduate ☐ 5

2nd ☐ 2   4th ☐ 4   graduate ☐ 6

21–24. Your expected enrollment status for the 1996–97 school year
(See Instructions, page 3.)

School term	Full time	3/4 time	1/2 time	Less than 1/2 time	Not enrolled
21. Summer term '96	☐ 1	☐ 2	☐ 3	☐ 4	☒ 5
22. Fall sem./quarter '96	☒ 1	☐ 2	☐ 3	☐ 4	☐ 5
23. Winter quarter '96–'97	☒ 1	☐ 2	☐ 3	☐ 4	☐ 5
24. Spring sem./quarter '97	☒ 1	☐ 2	☐ 3	☐ 4	☐ 5

25–26. Your degree/certificate and course of study
(See Instructions, page 3.)

25. Degree/certificate

26. Course of study   2 1

27. Date you expect to complete your degree/certificate   0 6   0 0
Month   Day   Year

28–30. In addition to grants, what other types of financial aid are you (and your parents) interested in?
(Check one or more boxes.)

• Work-study   ☒ 1

• Student loans   ☒ 2

• Parent loans for students (Federal PLUS)   ☒ 3

31. If you are (or were) in college, do you plan to attend **that same college** in 1996–97?

Yes ☐ 1   No ☐ 2

32. For how many dependent children will you pay child care expenses in 1996–97?

33–34. Veterans education benefits you expect to receive from July 1, 1996, through June 30, 1997

33. Amount per month $_____.00

34. Number of months

Section C: Education Background

35–36. Date that you (the student) received, or will receive, your high school diploma, either—

- by graduating from high school

    | 0 6 | 9 6 |
    | Month | Year |

    OR

- by earning a GED

    | | | | |
    | Month | Year |

    (Enter one date. Leave blank if the question does not apply to you.)

37–38. Highest grade level completed by your father and your mother *(Check one box for each parent. See Instructions, page 4.)*

	37. Father	38. Mother
elementary school (K–8)	☐₁	☐₁
high school (9–12)	☒₂	☒₂
college or beyond	☐₃	☐₃
unknown	☐₄	☐₄

Section D: Federal Family Education Loan (FFEL) Program Information

(Leave this section blank if you have never received a Federal Stafford Loan, a guaranteed student loan [GSL], or a Federal Insured Student Loan [FISL].)

39. If you borrowed under the Federal Stafford, Federal SLS, Federal PLUS, or Federal Consolidation Loan program and there is an outstanding balance on your loan(s), enter the date of your oldest outstanding loan.

| | | | |
| Month | Year |

42. Check one box to indicate the interest rate you have on your outstanding Federal Stafford Loan.

7% ☐₁   9% ☐₃   Variable ☐₅

8% ☐₂   8%/10% ☐₄

40–41. Write in the total outstanding balance(s) on your Federal Stafford and Federal SLS Loans.

Amount owed

40. Federal Stafford Loan(s) $_____.00

41. Federal SLS Loan(s) $_____.00

43–44. Do you currently have a Federal PLUS Loan or a Consolidation Loan?

	Yes	No
43. Federal PLUS Loan	☐₁	☐₂
44. Federal Consolidation Loan	☐₁	☐₂

Section E: Student Status

	Yes	No
45. Were you born **before** January 1, 1973?	☐₁	☒₂
46. Are you a veteran of the U.S. Armed Forces?	☐₁	☒₂
47. Will you be a graduate or professional student in 1996–97?	☐₁	☒₂
48. Are you married?	☐₁	☒₂
49. Are you a ward of the court or are both your parents dead?	☐₁	☒₂
50. Do you have legal dependents *(other than a spouse)* that fit the definition in Instructions, page 4?	☐₁	☒₂

If you answered **"Yes"** to **any** question in Section E, go to Section F and fill out the **GRAY** and the **WHITE** areas on the rest of the form.

If you answered **"No"** to **every** question in Section E, go to Section F, and fill out the **BLUE** and the **WHITE** areas on the rest of the form.

Section F: Household Information

If you are filling out the GRAY and WHITE areas, answer questions 51 and 52, and go to Section G.

If you are filling out the BLUE and WHITE areas, skip questions 51 and 52. Answer questions 53 through 57 about your parents, and then go on to Section G.

STUDENT (& SPOUSE)

51. Number of family members in 1996–97 (Include yourself and your spouse. Include your children and other people only if they meet the definition in Instructions, page 5.) | | |

52. Number of college students in 1996–97 (Of the number in 51, how many will be in college at least half-time for at least one term? Include yourself. See Instructions, page 5.) | |

PARENTS

53. Your parents' current marital status:

single ☐₁   separated ☐₃   widowed ☐₅

married ☐₂   divorced ☒₄

54. Your parents' state of legal residence | O H |

55. Date your parent(s) became legal resident(s) of the state in question 54 *(See Instructions, page 5.)*

| 0 4 | | | 5 5 |
| Month | Day | Year |

56. Number of family members in 1996–97 (Include yourself and your parents. Include your parents' other children and other people only if they meet the definition in Instructions, page 5.) | 0 4 |

57. Number of college students in 1996–97 (Of the number in 56, how many will be in college at least half-time for at least one term? Include yourself. See Instructions, page 6.) | 1 |

Section G: 1995 Income, Earnings, and Benefits   Everyone must fill out the Student (& Spouse) column.   *Page 3*
(You must see the instructions for income and taxes that you should exclude from questions in this section.)

STUDENT (& SPOUSE)	**PARENTS**
58. The following 1995 U.S. income tax figures are from: *(Check only one box.)*	69. The following 1995 U.S. income tax figures are from: *(Check only one box.)*

a completed 1995 IRS Form 1040A or 1040EZ   (Go to 59) ☒₁   a completed 1995 IRS Form 1040A or 1040EZ (Go to 70) ☒₁

a completed 1995 IRS Form 1040   (Go to 59) ☐₂   a completed 1995 IRS Form 1040   (Go to 70) ☐₂

an estimated 1995 IRS Form 1040A or 1040EZ   (Go to 59) ☐₃   an estimated 1995 IRS Form 1040A or 1040EZ (Go to 70) ☐₃

an estimated 1995 IRS Form 1040   (Go to 59) ☐₄   an estimated 1995 IRS Form 1040   (Go to 70) ☐₄

A U.S. income tax return will not be filed.   (Skip to 62) ☐₅   A U.S. income tax return will not be filed.   (Skip to 73) ☐₅

1995 total number of exemptions (Form 1040-line 6e, or 1040A-line 6e; 1040EZ filers—*see Instructions, pages 6 & 7*.)   **59.** | 0 0 | **70.** | 0 4 |

1995 Adjusted Gross Income (AGI-Form 1040-line 31, 1040A-line 16, or 1040EZ-line 4, or *see Instructions, pages 6 & 7*.)   **60.** $ 1,200 .00   — **TAX FILERS ONLY** — **71.** $ 27,356 .00

1995 U.S. income tax paid (Form 1040-line 46, 1040A-line 25, or 1040EZ-line 8)   **61.** $ 0 .00   **72.** $ 2,284 .00

1995 Income earned from work   Student **62.** $ 1,200 .00   Father **73.** $_____.00

1995 Income earned from work   Spouse **63.** $_____.00   Mother **74.** $ 27,356 .00

1995 Untaxed income and benefits (yearly totals only)

  Social security benefits   **64.** $_____.00   **75.** $_____.00

  Aid to Families with Dependent Children (AFDC or ADC)   **65.** $_____.00   **76.** $_____.00

  Child support received for all children   **66.** $_____.00   **77.** $_____.00

  Other untaxed income and benefits from Worksheet #2, page 11   **67.** $_____.00   **78.** $ 1,890 .00

1995 Title IV Income Exclusions from Worksheet #3, page 12   **68.** $_____.00   **79.** $_____.00

Section H: Information Release

80-91. What college(s) do you plan to attend in 1996–97?
(Note: By answering this question, you are giving permission to send your application data to the college(s) you list below.)

Housing codes	1 = on-campus 3 = with parent(s)
	2 = off-campus 4 = with relative(s) other than parent(s)

	College name	Address (or code, see Instructions, page 7)	City	State	Housing codes
80.					**81.**
82.					**83.**
84.					**85.**
86.					**87.**
88.					**89.**
90.					**91.**

92. Do you give the U.S. Department of Education permission to send information from this form to the financial aid agencies in your state as well as to the state agencies of all of the colleges listed above?   Yes ☐₁ No ☐₂
(States and colleges may require additional information and may have their own deadlines for applying for financial aid. Be sure to see "Deadlines for State Student Aid" in Instructions, page 10.)

93. Check this box if you give Selective Service permission to register you. *(See Instructions, page 8.)*   ☐₁

94–95. Read and Sign

Page 4

Certification: All of the information provided by me or any other person on this form and in Section I, if completed, is true and complete to the best of my knowledge. I understand that this application is being filed jointly by all signatories. If asked by an authorized official, I agree to give proof of the information that I have given on this form and in Section I, if completed. I realize that this proof may include a copy of my U.S., state, or local income tax return. I also realize that if I do not give proof when asked, the student may be denied aid.

94. Everyone giving information on this form must sign below.
   If you do not sign this form, it will be returned unprocessed.

1 Student _____

2 Student's spouse _____

3 Father/Stepfather _____

4 Mother/Stepmother _____

95. Date completed | 0 1 | | 0 7 | Year   1996 ☒
           Month   Day   1997 ☐

School Use Only
Dependency override: enter 1   ⌐
Title IV Inst. Number
FAA signature: 1

MDE Use Only   Spec.   No.
(Do not write in this box.)   handle   copies

If you (and your family) have unusual circumstances, such as:

- tuition expenses at an elementary or secondary school,
- unusual medical or dental expenses, not covered by insurance,
- a family member who is a dislocated worker, or
- other unusual circumstances that might affect your eligibility for student financial aid, you should—
  Check with the financial aid office at your college.

Preparer's Use Only   *(For preparers other than student and parents. Student and parents, sign above. See Instructions, page 8.)*

Preparer's name

_____
Last   First   M.I.

Firm's name and address (or preparer's, if self-employed)

_____
Firm name

_____
Number and street (Include apt. no.)

_____
City   State   ZIP code

96. Employer identification number (EIN)

97. Preparer's social security number

Certification:
All of the information on this form and in Section I, if completed, is true and complete to the best of my knowledge.

98. Preparer's signature   **Date**

———————————— *ATTENTION* ————————————

If you are filling out the **GRAY and WHITE** areas, go to Instructions, page 8, and complete **WORKSHEET A. This will tell you whether you must fill out Section I. If you meet certain tax filing and income conditions, you may skip Section I.**

If you are filling out the **BLUE and WHITE** areas, go to Instructions, page 8, and complete **WORKSHEET B. This will tell you whether you must fill out Section I. If you meet certain tax filing and income conditions, you may skip Section I.**

Section I: Asset Information

	STUDENT (& SPOUSE)		PARENTS	
		106. Age of your older parent		
Cash, savings, and checking accounts	**99.** $_____85_____.00		**107.** $_____500_____.00	
Other real estate and investments value *(Don't include the home.)*	**100.** $_____0_____.00		**108.** $_____0_____.00	
Other real estate and investments debt *(Don't include the home.)*	**101.** $_____0_____.00		**109.** $_____0_____.00	
Business value	**102.** $_____0_____.00		**110.** $_____0_____.00	
Business debt	**103.** $_____0_____.00		**111.** $_____0_____.00	
Farm value *(See Instructions, pages 8 & 9.)*	**104.** $_____0_____.00		**112.** $_____0_____.00	
Farm debt *(See Instructions, pages 8 & 9.)*	**105.** $_____0_____.00		**113.** $_____0_____.00	

MAKE SURE THAT YOU HAVE COMPLETED, DATED, AND SIGNED THE APPLICATION.
Mail the application to: Federal Student Aid Programs, P.O. Box 4016, Iowa City, IA 52243-4016.

Financial Aid *P*ROFILE — 1996-97

Michael Twofer
CSS No. 2345678
222-22-2222

Complete all sections of the PROFILE Form except Section E. Be certain that everyone giving information on the form signs it.

Section A — Student's Information

1. How many family members will the student (and spouse) support in 1996-97? List their names and give information about them in M. See instructions. `0`

2. Of the number in 1, how many will be in college at least half-time for at least one term in 1996-97? Include yourself. `0 0`

3. What is the student's state of legal residence? `O H`

4. What is the student's citizenship status?

a. 1 ☒ U.S. citizen

2 ☐ Permanent resident

3 ☐ Neither of the above (Answer "b" and "c" below.)

b. Country of citizenship?

c. Visa classification?

1 ☐ F1 2 ☐ F2 3 ☐ J1 4 ☐ J2 5 ☐ Other

Section B — Student's 1995 Income & Benefits

Don't report parents' information on this page. If married, include spouse's information in Sections B, C, D, and E.

5. The following 1995 U.S. Income tax return figures are (Mark only one box.)

1 ☒ estimated. Will file IRS Form 1040EZ or 1040A. Go to 6.

2 ☐ estimated. Will file IRS Form 1040. Go to 6.

3 ☐ from a completed IRS Form 1040EZ or 1040A. Go to 6.

4 ☐ from a completed IRS Form 1040. Go to 6.

5 ☐ a tax return will not be filed. Skip to 10.

Tax Filers Only

6. 1995 total number of exemptions (IRS Form 1040, line 6e or 1040A, line 6e or 1040EZ — see instructions) **6.** `0 0`

7. 1995 Adjusted Gross Income from IRS Form 1040, line 31 or 1040A, line 13 or 1040EZ, line 3 (Use the worksheet in the instructions.) **7.** $ `1,200` .00

8. 1995 U.S. income tax paid (IRS Form 1040, line 47 or 1040A, line 22 or 1040EZ, line 9) **8.** $ `0` .00

9. 1995 itemized deductions (IRS Form 1040, Schedule A, line 26. Write in "0" if deductions were not itemized.) **9.** $ `0` .00

10. 1995 income earned from work by student (See instructions.) **10.** $ `1,200` .00

11. 1995 income earned from work by student's spouse **11.** $ .00

12. 1995 dividend and interest income **12.** $ `0` .00

13. 1995 untaxed income and benefits (Give total amount for the year.)

a. Social security benefits (See instructions.) **13. a.** $ `0` .00

b. Aid to Families with Dependent Children **b.** $ `0` .00

c. Child support received for all the student's children **c.** $ `0` .00

d. Earned Income Credit (IRS Form 1040, line 56 or 1040A, line 28c) **d.** $ `0` .00

e. Other – write total from worksheet, page X. **e.** $ `0` .00

14. 1995 earnings from Federal Work-Study or other need-based work programs plus any grant and scholarship aid in excess of tuition, fees, books, and supplies **14.** $ `0` .00

Section C — Student's Assets

15. Cash, savings, and checking accounts $ `85.00`

	What is it worth today?	What is owed on it?
16. Investments (Including Uniform Gifts to Minors. See instructions.)	$ `0` .00	$ .00
17. Home (Renters write in "0.")	$ `0` .00	$ .00
18. Other real estate	$ `0` .00	$ .00
19. Business and farm	$ `0` .00	$ .00

20. If the farm is included in 19, is the student living on the farm? Yes ☐ 1 No ☐ 2

21. If student owns home, give

a. year purchased `1 9` b. purchase price $ .00

Section D — Student's Trust Information

22. a. Total value of all trust(s) $ `0` .00

b. Is any income or part of the principal currently available? Yes ☐ 1 No ☐ 2

c. Who established the trust(s)?

1 ☐ Student's parents 2 ☐ Other

Section E — Student's Expenses

23. 1995 child support paid by student $ `0` .00

24. 1995 medical and dental expenses not covered by insurance (See instructions.) $ `0` .00

Section F — Student's Expected Summer/School-Year Resources for 1996-97

	Amount per month	Number of months
25. Student's veterans benefits (July 1, 1996 – June 30, 1997)	$ _____ .00	⊔⊔

26. Student's (and spouse's) resources
(Don't enter monthly amounts.)

	Summer 1996 (3 months)	School Year 1996-97 (9 months)
a. Student's wages, salaries, tips, etc.	$ 1,200 .00	$ 0 .00
b. Spouse's wages, salaries, tips, etc.	$ 0 .00	$ 0 .00
c. Other taxable income	$ 0 .00	$ 0 .00
d. Untaxed income and benefits	$ 0 .00	$ 0 .00
e. Grants, scholarships, fellowships, etc. from other than the colleges to which the student is applying (List sources in Section P.)		$ 0 .00
f. Tuition benefits from the parents' and/or the student's or spouse's employer		$ 0 .00
g. Contributions from the student's parent(s)		$ 0 .00
h. Contributions from other relatives, spouse's parents, and all other sources		$ 0 .00

Section G — Parents' Household Information – See page X of the instruction booklet.

27. How many family members will your parents support in 1996-97? Always include yourself (the student). List their names and give information about them in M. |0,4|

28. Of the number in 27, how many will be in college at least half-time for at least one term in 1996-97? Include the student. |1|

29. How many parents will be in college at least half-time in 1996-97? (Mark only one box.)
1 ☒Neither parent   2 ☐ One parent   3 ☐ Both parents

30. What is the current marital status of your parents? (Mark only one box.)
1 ☐ single   3 ☐ separated   5 ☐ widowed
2 ☐ married   4 ☒ divorced

31. What is your parents' state of legal residence? |b,H|

Section H — Parents' Expenses

	1995	Expected 1996
32. Child support paid by the parent(s) completing this form	32 a. $ 0 .00	32. b. $ 0 .00
33. Repayment of educational loans (See instructions.)	33 a. $ 0 .00	33. b. $ 0 .00
34. Medical and dental expenses not covered by insurance (See instructions.)	34 a. $ 0 .00	34. b. $ 0 .00

35. Total elementary, junior high school, and high school tuition paid for dependent children

Amount paid (Don't include tuition paid for the student.)	35 a. $ 0 .00	35c. $ 0 .00
For how many dependent children? (Don't include the student.)	b. ⊔	d. ⊔

Section I — Parents' Assets – If parents own all or part of a business or farm, write in its name and the percent of ownership in Section P.

36. Cash, savings, and checking accounts	$ 500 .00
37. Monthly home mortgage or rental payment (If none, explain in Section P.)	$ 535 .00

	What is it worth today?	What is owed on it?
38. Investments	$ 0 .00	$ _____ .00
39a. Home (Renters write in "0.")	$ 0 .00	$ _____ .00
b. year purchased |1,9,,| c. purchase price $ _____ .00		

	What is it worth today?	What is owed on it?
40. Business	$ _____ .00	$ _____ .00
41. a. Farm	$ _____ .00	$ _____ .00
b. Does family live on the farm? Yes ☐1 No ☐2		
42. a. Other real estate	$ 0 .00	$ _____ .00
b. year purchased |1,9,,| c. purchase price $ _____ .00		

PROFILE — 1996-97

Section J — Parents' 1994 Income and Benefits

43. 1994 Adjusted Gross Income (IRS Form 1040, line 31 or 1040A, line 13 or 1040EZ, line 3) $ 25,218 .00

44. 1994 U.S. Income tax paid (IRS Form 1040, line 47, 1040A, line 22 or 1040EZ, line 9) $ 1,951 .00

45. 1994 itemized deductions (IRS Form 1040, Schedule A, line 26. Write "0" if deductions were not itemized) $ 0 .00

46. 1994 untaxed income and benefits (Include the same types of income & benefits that are listed in 53 a – k.) $ 12,690 .00

Section K — Parents' 1995 Income & Benefits

47. The following 1995 U.S. income tax return figures are (Mark only one box.)

1 ☐ estimated. Will file IRS Form 1040EZ or 1040A. Go to 48.   2 ☒ estimated. Will file IRS Form 1040. Go to 48.   3 ☐ from a completed IRS Form 1040EZ or 1040A. Go to 48.   4 ☐ from a completed IRS Form 1040. Go to 48.   5 ☐ a tax return will not be filed. Skip to 52.

Tax Filers Only

48. 1995 total number of exemptions (IRS Form 1040, line 6e or 1040A, line 6e or 1040EZ)   **48.** | 0 | 4 |

49. 1995 Adjusted Gross Income (IRS Form 1040, line 31 or 1040A, line 13 or 1040EZ, line 3)   **49.** $ 27,356 .00

Breakdown of income in 49

a. Wages, salaries, tips (IRS Form 1040, line 7 or 1040A, line 7 or 1040EZ, line 1)   **49 a.** $ 27,356 .00

b. Interest income (IRS Form 1040, line 8a or 1040A, line 8a or 1040EZ, line 2)   **b.** $ .00

c. Dividend income (IRS Form 1040, line 9 or 1040A, line 9)   **c.** $ .00

d. Net income (or loss) from business, farm, rents, royalties, partnerships, estates, trusts, etc. (IRS Form 1040, lines 12, 18, and 19) If a loss, enter the amount in (parentheses).   **d.** $ .00

e. Other taxable income such as alimony received, capital gains (or losses), pensions, annuities, etc. (IRS Form 1040, lines 10, 11, 13-15, 16b, 17b, 20, 21b, and 22 or 1040A, line 10)   **e.** $ .00

f. Adjustments to income (IRS Form 1040, line 30 or 1040A, line 12c)   **f.** $ .00

50. 1995 U.S. income tax paid (IRS Form 1040, line 47, 1040A, line 22 or 1040EZ, line 9)   **50.** $ 2,284 .00

51. 1995 itemized deductions (IRS Form 1040, Schedule A, line 26. Write in "0" if deductions were not itemized.)   **51.** $ 0 .00

52. 1995 Income earned from work by father   **52.** $ .00

53. 1995 Income earned from work by mother   **53.** $ 27,356 .00

54. 1995 untaxed income and benefits (Give total amount for the year. Do not give monthly amounts.)

a. Social security benefits   **54a.** $ .00

b. Aid to Families with Dependent Children   **b.** $ .00

c. Child support received for all children   **c.** $ 10,800 .00

d. Deductible IRA and/or Keogh payments (See instructions.)   **d.** $ .00

e. Payments to tax-deferred pension and savings plans (See instructions.)   **e.** $ .00

f. Amounts withheld from wages for dependent care and medical spending accounts   **f.** $ .00

g. Earned Income Credit (IRS Form 1040, line 56 or 1040A, line 28c)   **g.** $ 1,890 .00

h. Housing, food and other living allowances (See instructions.)   **h.** $ .00

i. Tax-exempt interest income (IRS Form 1040, line 8b or 1040A, line 8b)   **i.** $ .00

j. Foreign income exclusion (IRS Form 2555, line 43)   **j.** $ .00

k. Other – write in the total from the worksheet in the instructions, page X.   **k.** $ .00

WRITE ONLY IN THE ANSWER SPACES. DO NOT WRITE ANYWHERE ELSE.

Section L — Parents' 1996 Expected Income & Benefits

(If the expected total income and benefits will differ from the 1995 total income and benefits by $3,000 or more, explain in P.)

55. 1996 income earned from work by father $ .00   **57.** 1996 other taxable income $ .00

56. 1996 income earned from work by mother $ 28,000 .00   **58.** 1996 untaxed income and benefits $ 12,000 .00

Section M —Family Member Listing

Give information for all family members but don't give information about yourself. List up to seven other family members here. If there are more than seven, list first those who will be in college at least half-time. List the others in Section P.

59.

Full name of family member / You — the student applicant	Age	Claimed as tax exemption in 1995? Yes?	No?	Use codes from below.	1995-96 school year Name of school or college	Year in school	Scholarships and grants	Parents' contribution	1996-97 school year Attend college at least one term full-time / half-time	Name of school or college
1									1☐ 2☐	
2 Tammy Twofer	51	☒	☐	1					1☐ 2☐	
3 Theresa Twofer	13	☒	☐	3					1☐ 2☐	
4 Matthew Twofer	11	☒	☐	3					1☐ 2☐	
5		☐	☐						1☐ 2☐	
6		☐	☐						1☐ 2☐	
7		☐	☐						1☐ 2☐	
8		☐	☐						1☐ 2☐	

Write in the correct code from the right. ↑   1 = Student's parent   3 = Student's brother or sister   5 = Student's son or daughter   7 = Other
2 = Student's stepparent   4 = Student's husband or wife   6 = Student's grandparent

Section N — Parents' Information

60. Mark one: ☐ Father   ☐ Stepfather   ☐ Legal guardian   ☐ Other (Explain in P.)

a. Name _____ Age ☐☐

b. Mark if: ☐ Self-employed   ☐ Unemployed – Date last employed: _____

c. Occupation _____

d. Employer _____ No. years _____

e. Work telephone (optional) ☐☐☐-☐☐☐-☐☐☐☐

f. Retirement plans: ☐ Social security   ☐ Union/employer   ☐ Civil service/state   ☐ IRA/Keogh/tax-deferred   ☐ Military   ☐ Other

61. Mark one: ☒ Mother   ☐ Stepmother   ☐ Legal guardian   ☐ Other (Explain in P.)

a. Name __Tammy Twofer__ Age 5 1

b. Mark if: ☐ Self-employed   ☐ Unemployed – Date last employed: _____

c. Occupation __Nurse__

d. Employer __Secondtown Hospital__ No. years 8

e. Work telephone (optional) ☐☐☐-☐☐☐-☐☐☐☐

f. Retirement plans: ☒ Social security only   ☒ Union/employer   ☐ Civil service/state   ☐ IRA/Keogh/tax-deferred   ☐ Military   ☐ Other

Section O — Divorced, Separated, or Remarried Parents

(To be answered by the parent who completes this form, if the student's natural or adoptive parents are divorced, separated, or remarried.)

62. a. Year of separation 8 7   Year of divorce 8 8

b. Other parent's name __Thomas Twofer__
Home address __Secondtown, OH__

Occupation/Employer __Physician__

c. According to court order, when will support for the student end? 0 2 / 9 6   Month   Year

d. Who last claimed the student as a tax exemption? __Mother__ Year? 9 5

e. How much does the other parent plan to contribute to the student's education for the 1995-96 school year? $ 0 .00

f. Is there an agreement specifying this contribution for the student's education? Yes ☐   No ☒

Section P — Explanations/Special Circumstances

Use this space to explain any unusual expenses such as high medical or dental expenses. educational and other debts, child care, elder care, or special circumstances. Also, give information for any outside scholarships you have been awarded.

Certification:

All the information on this form is true and complete to the best of my knowledge. If asked, I agree to give proof of the information that I have given on this form. I realize that this proof may include a copy of my U.S., state, or local income tax returns. I certify that all information is correct at this time, and that I will send timely notice of any significant change in family income or assets, financial situation, college plans of other children, or the receipt of other scholarships or grants.

1 _____
Student's signature

2 _____
Student's spouse's signature

3 _____
Father's (stepfather's) signature

4 _____
Mother's (stepmother's) signature

Date this form was completed:
☐☐ ☐☐   1☐ 1995
Month   Day   2☐ 1996
     3☐ 1997
     Year

DIVORCED/SEPARATED PARENT'S STATEMENT
School Year 1996-97

Section I — Student Applicant Information

1. a. Student's name: T W O F E R (Last)   M I C H A E L (First)   (M.I.)

b. Student's social security number: 2 22 – 2 2 – 2 2 2 2

Section II — Parent's (and Current Spouse's) Information

2. Student's parent

a. Name: Thomas Twofer   **b.** Age: 56

c. Street address: 2020 Duodenum

City, State, Zip code: Secondtown, OH

d. Occupation: Physician

e. Title: _____

f. Employer: Self

g. Number of years with employer: 30

h. Are you covered by this employer's pension plan? yes ☐ no ☐

i. State of legal residence: OH

j. Social security number: ___ – __ – ____

3. Parent's current spouse (if any)

a. Name: Tiffany Twofer   **b.** Age: 35

c. Street address: Same

City, State, Zip code: _____

d. Occupation: None

e. Title: _____

f. Employer: _____

g. Number of years with employer: _____

h. Are you covered by this employer's pension plan? yes ☐ no ☐

i. State of legal residence: _____

j. Social security number: ___ – __ – ____

4. Parent's support of former household

a. Name of person who claimed student as a dependent on most recent U.S. income tax return: _____

	1995	1996
b. Annual child support paid for all children	$ 7,200 00	$ 4,200 00
c. Annual child support paid for the student applicant	$ 3,600 00	600 00

d. When will (did) student applicant's support end? Feb. 1984

e. Alimony paid	$ 0 00	$ 0 00
f. What do you expect to contribute to the student applicant's education in addition to child support?	$ 0 00	$ 0 00

Parent's current household

5. Total number of exemptions claimed or expected to be claimed on parent's U.S. income tax return for

1995: 2   1996: 2

6. Total size of the parent's household during 1996-97 (Include the parent, the parent's current spouse (if any) and parent's other dependent children. Include other dependents if they meet the definition in the instructions.) — 0 2

7. Of the number in 6, how many will be in college during 1996-97? (Include only persons who will be enrolled at least half-time.) — 2

8. Give information for all individuals included in parent's household in 6. Include the parent and the parent's current spouse (if any). For persons not in school, provide name and age only.

Name	Age	Educational Information 1995-96						Educational Information 1996-97			
		Name of school or college, 1995-96	Year in school or college	Tuition and fees	Room and board	Scholarships and gift aid	Parent's contribution	Name of school or college, 1996-97	full-time	half-time or more	less than half-time
Thomas Twofer	56										
Tiffany Twofer	35										

If more space is needed, continue in Section V, "Remarks."

Section III — Parent's (and Current Spouse's) Annual Income and Expenses

9. Total taxable income (See instructions.) The following income figures are:

☐ from a completed 1995 IRS Form 1040A or 1040EZ.   ☐ from a completed 1995 IRS Form 1040.   ☐ estimated, a 1995 tax return will be filed.   ☐ estimated, a tax return **will not** be filed.

	Total 1995	Estimated 1996
a. Wages, salaries, tips, and other compensation		
(1) Student's parent	$ 83,260 00	$ 85,000 00
(2) Parent's current spouse	$ 0 00	$ 0 00
b. Interest income	$ 3,817 00	$ 4,000 00
c. Dividends	$ 7,378 00	$ 7,000 00
d. Net income (or loss) from business or farm. If negative, enter amount in (parentheses)	$ 0 00	$ 0 00

For questions 9e and 9f, list kinds and amounts in Section V, "Remarks."

e. All other taxable income	$ 0 00	$ 0 00
f. Adjustments to income	$ 0 00	$ 0 00

Section III — Parent's (and Current Spouse's) Annual Income and Expenses (continued)

	Total 1995	Estimated 1996
10. Total **nontaxable income** (See instructions.)		
a. Untaxed social security benefits	$ 0 00	$ 0 00
b. All other income — child support received, welfare benefits, veterans benefits, housing allowances, etc. (List kinds and amounts in Section V, "Remarks.")	$ 0 00	$ 0 00

Expenses (See instructions.)

	Total 1995		Total 1995
11. U.S. income tax paid	$ 24,494 00	**14.** Medical and dental expenses not paid by insurance	$_____ 00
12. IRS itemized deductions, if applicable	$ 16,355 00	**15.** Other unusual expenses (List kinds and amounts in Section V, "Remarks.")	$_____ 00
13. State and local taxes	$ 4,240 00		

Section IV — Parent's (and Current Spouse's) Assets and Debts

16. a. Housing payment (Check one.) ☐ rent ☐ mortgage

b. Monthly amount (If zero, explain in Section V, "Remarks.") $ 1,055 00

	Year purchased	Purchase price	Present market value	Unpaid mortgage principal
17. Home—if owned or being purchased	1987	$ 180,000 00	$ 165,000 00	$ 109,000 00
18. Other real estate	None	$_____ 00	$_____ 00	$_____ 00
19. Cash, savings, checking accounts, and bonds		$ 36,000 00		
20. Investments—net value of stocks and other securities (List kinds and amounts in Section V, "Remarks.")		$ 165,000 00		
21. Business and/or farm	**a.** Present market value	$ N/A 00		
	b. Indebtedness	$_____ 00		
	c. Percent of ownership	_____%		
22. Other debts outstanding (Do **not** include any debts entered above. List kinds, purposes, and amounts in Section V, "Remarks.")		$_____ 00		

Section V — Remarks

Section VI — Certification and Authorization

I declare that the information reported on this form is true, correct, and complete.

I agree that, to verify information reported on this form, I will on request provide an official copy of my state or U.S. income tax return.

I further agree to provide, if requested, any other official documentation necessary to verify information reported.

Student applicant's parent's signature

_____

Date completed _____

▶ Do you authorize the college to discuss the information outlined on this form with the student applicant?

yes ☐   no ☐

21823-01582 • S83M95 • 236202

college. Tammy's assets are $500 in her checking account. As a single parent age 51, she can protect (Table 6) $29,400 of her assets. That means she has a big round zero in assets available for college. And her total available funds are the $3,652 left from her income.

Applying the final step of the formula from Table 7, we see Tammy is expected to contribute just $803 to Michael's first year at college. If Michael's parents were still married and his father's income and assets figured in the formula, the parental contribution would be 10 times that amount.

The $1,200 Michael earned last year is less than the automatic $1,750 deduction for dependent students. So he's expected to contribute nothing.

Michael's EFC is the amount Mom is expected to pay, a very low $803. It guarantees him a high magic number almost wherever he goes.

MELISSA THREEBY

Melissa lives in Thirdburg, Oregon. Her parents, John and Maria Threeby, were married just out of high school. Melissa was born when her mother was 18. John got a job as a used car salesman and worked his way up to sales manager at a Thirdburg auto dealership. Maria took some real estate classes and now works full time as a realtor. In addition to Melissa, they have a son in 10th grade.

Last year Melissa's father earned $67,805. Her mother made $33,118. Together they earn less than Michael's parents but because they are married, Melissa won't fare as well as Michael on the FAFSA. Melissa's parents have acquired stocks, bonds, and other investments worth $83,500.

Melissa earns spending money as a waitress at the Third Cafe. Last year, she made $2,674. She keeps her unspent money in an interest-paying checking account. At the time she applied for aid, she had $500 in the bank.

(Continued on page 108)

Free Application for Federal Student Aid

F F F F F

WARNING: If you purposely give false or misleading information on
this form, you may be fined $10,000, sent to prison, or both.
"You" and "your" on this form always mean the student who wants aid.

Form Approved
OMB No. 1840-0110
APP. EXP: 6/30/97

U.S. Department of Education
Student Financial
Assistance Programs

Section A: Yourself

1–3. Your name   T H R E E BY   M E L I S S A
                                      1. Last   **2. First**   **3. M.I.**

     Your title (optional)   Mr. ☐ 1   Miss, Ms., or Mrs. ☐ 2

4–7. Your permanent mailing address   3 3 3   T H I R D   WA Y
       (*All mail will be sent to this*   **4. Number and street (Include apt. no.)**
       address. See Instructions, page 2   T H I R D B UR G   O R   3 3 3 3 3
       for state/country abbreviations.)   **5. City**   **6. State**   **7. ZIP code**

8. Your permanent home   5 0 3 5 5 5 1 2 12
     telephone number   Area code

9. Your state of legal residence   O R
                                         State

10. Date you became a legal resident of the state in question 9
     (*See Instructions, page 2.*)   0 3   2 3   7 6
                                 Month   Day   Year

11–12. Your driver's license number (*Include the state abbreviation. If
you don't have a license, leave this question blank.*)

       State

13. Your social security number   3 3 3 3 3 3 3 33 3
     (*Don't leave blank. See Instructions, page 3.*)

14. Your date of birth   0 3 2 3   7 6
                        Month   Day   Year

15–16. Are you a U.S. citizen? (*See Instructions, page 3.*)

     Yes, I am a U.S. citizen.   ☒ 1

     No, but I am an eligible noncitizen.   ☐ 2

     A

     No, neither of the above.   ☐ 3

17. As of **today**, are you married? (*Check only one box.*)

     I am not married. (I am single,   ☒ 1
     widowed, or divorced.)

     I am married.   ☐ 2

     I am separated from my spouse.   ☐ 3

18. Date you were married, widowed, separated,
or divorced. If divorced, use earliest
date of divorce or separation.   Month   Year

19. Will you have your first bachelor's
degree before July 1, 1996?   Yes ☐ 1   No ☒ 2

Section B: Your Plans

20. Your year in college during the 1996–97 school year
     (*Check only one box.*)
     1st ☒ 1   3rd ☐ 3   5th year or more undergraduate ☐ 5
     2nd ☐ 2   4th ☐ 4   graduate   ☐ 6

21–24. Your expected enrollment status for the 1996–97 school year
     (*See Instructions, page 3.*)

School term	Full time	3/4 time	1/2 time	Less than 1/2 time	Not enrolled
21. Summer term '96	☐ 1	☐ 2	☐ 3	☐ 4	☒ 5
22. Fall sem./quarter '96	☒ 1	☐ 2	☐ 3	☐ 4	☐ 5
23. Winter quarter '96–'97	☒ 1	☐ 2	☐ 3	☐ 4	☐ 5
24. Spring sem./quarter '97	☒ 1	☐ 2	☐ 3	☐ 4	☐ 5

25–26. Your degree/certificate   **25.** Degree/certificate
and course of study
(*See Instructions, page 3.*)   **26.** Course of study   1 1

27. Date you expect to complete   0 6   0 0
your degree/certificate   Month   Day   Year

28–30. In addition to grants, what other types of financial
aid are you (and your parents) interested in?
(*Check one or more boxes.*)

     • Work-study   ☒ 1

     • Student loans   ☒ 2

     • Parent loans for students (Federal PLUS) ☒ 3

31. If you are (or were) in college, do you plan
to attend **that same college** in 1996–97?

                        Yes ☐ 1   No ☐ 2

32. For how many dependent children will you
pay child care expenses in 1996–97?

33–34. Veterans education benefits you expect to
receive from July 1, 1996, through June 30, 1997

     33. Amount per month $_____.00

     34. Number of months

Section C: Education Background

35–36. Date that you (the student) received, or will receive, your high school diploma, either—

- by graduating from high school `0 6` `9 6`
  Month Year

  OR

- by earning a GED `|   |` `|   |`
  Month Year

(Enter one date. Leave blank if the question does not apply to you.)

37–38. Highest grade level completed by your father and your mother *(Check one box for each parent. See Instructions, page 4.)*

	37. Father	**38.** Mother
elementary school (K–8)	☐₁	☐₁
high school (9–12)	☐₂	☐₂
college or beyond	☒₃	☒₃
unknown	☐₄	☐₄

Section D: Federal Family Education Loan (FFEL) Program Information

(Leave this section blank if you have never received a Federal Stafford Loan, a guaranteed student loan [GSL], or a Federal Insured Student Loan [FISL].)

39. If you borrowed under the Federal Stafford, Federal SLS, Federal PLUS, or Federal Consolidation Loan program and there is an outstanding balance on your loan(s), enter the date of your oldest outstanding loan.

`|   |` `|   |`
Month Year

40–41. Write in the total outstanding balance(s) on your Federal Stafford and Federal SLS Loans.

Amount owed

40. Federal Stafford Loan(s) $_____.00

41. Federal SLS Loan(s) $_____.00

42. Check one box to indicate the interest rate you have on your outstanding Federal Stafford Loan.

7% ☐₁ 9% ☐₃ Variable ☐₅

8% ☐₂ 8%/10% ☐₄

43–44. Do you currently have a Federal PLUS Loan or a Consolidation Loan?

	Yes	No
43. Federal PLUS Loan	☐₁	☐₂
44. Federal Consolidation Loan	☐₁	☐₂

Section E: Student Status

	Yes	No
45. Were you born **before** January 1, 1973?	☐₁	☒₂
46. Are you a veteran of the U.S. Armed Forces?	☐₁	☒₂
47. Will you be a graduate or professional student in 1996–97?	☐₁	☒₂
48. Are you married?	☐₁	☒₂
49. Are you a ward of the court or are both your parents dead?	☐₁	☒₂
50. Do you have legal dependents *(other than a spouse)* that fit the definition in Instructions, page 4?	☐₁	☒₂

If you answered **"Yes"** to **any** question in Section E, go to Section F and fill out the **GRAY** and the **WHITE** areas on the rest of the form.

If you answered **"No"** to **every** question in Section E, go to Section F, and fill out the **BLUE** and the **WHITE** areas on the rest of the form.

Section F: Household Information

If you are filling out the **GRAY** and **WHITE** areas, answer questions 51 and 52, and go to Section G.

If you are filling out the **BLUE** and **WHITE** areas, skip questions 51 and 52. Answer questions 53 through 57 about your parents, and then go on to Section G.

STUDENT (& SPOUSE)

51. Number of family members in 1996–97 (Include yourself and your spouse. Include your children and other people only if they meet the definition in Instructions, page 5.) `|   |`

52. Number of college students in 1996–97 (Of the number in 51, how many will be in college at least half-time for at least one term? Include yourself. *See Instructions, page 5.*) `|   |`

PARENTS

53. Your parents' current marital status:

single ☐₁ separated ☐₃ widowed ☐₅

married ☒₂ divorced ☐₄

54. Your parents' state of legal residence `O R`

55. Date your parent(s) became legal resident(s) of the state in question 54 `0 5` `|   |` `6 9`
(See Instructions, page 5.) Month Day Year

56. Number of family members in 1996–97 (Include yourself and your parents. Include your parents' other children and other people only if they meet the definition in Instructions, page 5.) `0 4`

57. Number of college students in 1996–97 (Of the number in 56, how many will be in college at least half-time for at least one term? Include yourself. *See Instructions, page 6.*) `1`

Section G: 1995 Income, Earnings, and Benefits   Everyone must fill out the Student (& Spouse) column.   *Page 3*

(You must see the instructions for income and taxes that you should exclude from questions in this section.)

STUDENT (& SPOUSE)

58. The following 1995 U.S. income tax figures are from:
    (Check only one box.)

a completed 1995 IRS Form 1040A or 1040EZ   (Go to 59)   [x]₁

a completed 1995 IRS Form 1040   (Go to 59)   ☐₂

an estimated 1995 IRS Form 1040A or 1040EZ   (Go to 59)   ☐₃

an estimated 1995 IRS Form 1040   (Go to 59)   ☐₄

A U.S. income tax return will not be filed.   (Skip to 62)   ☐₅

PARENTS

69. The following 1995 U.S. income tax figures are from:
    (Check only one box.)

a completed 1995 IRS Form 1040A or 1040EZ (Go to 70)   ☐₁

a completed 1995 IRS Form 1040   (Go to 70)   [x]₂

an estimated 1995 IRS Form 1040A or 1040EZ (Go to 70)   ☐₃

an estimated 1995 IRS Form 1040   (Go to 70)   ☐₄

A U.S. income tax return will not be filed.   (Skip to 73)   ☐₅

1995 total number of exemptions (Form 1040-line 6e, or 1040A-line 6e; 1040EZ filers—*see Instructions, pages 6 & 7*.)   **59.**   0   0   **70.**   0   4

1995 Adjusted Gross Income (AGI-Form 1040-line 31, 1040A-line 16, or 1040EZ-line 4, or *see Instructions, pages 6 & 7*.)   **60.** $ 2,677 .00 — **TAX FILERS ONLY** — **71.** $ 101,581 .00

1995 U.S. income tax paid (Form 1040-line 46, 1040A-line 25, or 1040EZ-line 8)   **61.** $ 0 .00   **72.** $ 19,837 .00

1995 Income earned from work   Student **62.** $ 2,674 .00   Father **73.** $ 67,805 .00

1995 Income earned from work   Spouse **63.** $_____ .00   Mother **74.** $ 33,118 .00

1995 Untaxed income and benefits (yearly totals only)

Social security benefits   **64.** $_____ .00   **75.** $_____ .00

Aid to Families with Dependent Children (AFDC or ADC)   **65.** $_____ .00   **76.** $_____ .00

Child support received for all children   **66.** $_____ .00   **77.** $_____ .00

Other untaxed income and benefits from Worksheet #2, page 11   **67.** $_____ .00   **78.** $_____ .00

1995 Title IV Income Exclusions from Worksheet #3, page 12   **68.** $_____ .00   **79.** $_____ .00

Section H: Information Release

80-91. What college(s) do you plan to attend in 1996–97?

Housing codes	1 = on-campus	3 = with parent(s)
	2 = off-campus	4 = with relative(s) other than parent(s)

(Note: By answering this question, you are giving permission to send your application data to the college(s) you list below.)

	College name	Address (or code, see Instructions, page 7)	City	State	Housing codes
80.					**81.**
82.					**83.**
84.					**85.**
86.					**87.**
88.					**89.**
90.					**91.**

92. Do you give the U.S. Department of Education permission to send information from this form to the financial aid agencies in your state as well as to the state agencies of all of the colleges listed above?   Yes ☐₁   No ☐₂

   (States and colleges may require additional information and may have their own deadlines for applying for financial aid. Be sure to see "Deadlines for State Student Aid" in Instructions, page 10.)

93. Check this box if you give Selective Service permission to register you. *(See Instructions, page 8.)*   ☐₁

94–95. Read and Sign

Page 4

Certification: All of the information provided by me or any other person on this form and in Section I, if completed, is true and complete to the best of my knowledge. I understand that this application is being filed jointly by all signatories. If asked by an authorized official, I agree to give proof of the information that I have given on this form and in Section I, if completed. I realize that this proof may include a copy of my U.S., state, or local income tax return. I also realize that if I do not give proof when asked, the student may be denied aid.

94. Everyone giving information on this form must sign below. If you do not sign this form, it will be returned unprocessed.

1 Student

2 Student's spouse

3 Father/Stepfather

4 Mother/Stepmother

95. Date completed | 0 1 | 0 7 | Year | 1996 [X]
Month   Day   1997 [ ]

School Use Only

Dependency override: enter 1 [ ]

Title IV Inst. Number

FAA signature: 1

MDE Use Only   Spec.   No.
(Do not write in this box.)   handle [ ]   copies [ ]

If you (and your family) have unusual circumstances, such as:

- tuition expenses at an elementary or secondary school,
- unusual medical or dental expenses, not covered by insurance,
- a family member who is a dislocated worker, or
- other unusual circumstances that might affect your eligibility for student financial aid, you should—
  Check with the financial aid office at your college.

Preparer's Use Only

(For preparers other than student and parents. Student and parents, sign above. See Instructions, page 8.)

Preparer's name

Last   First   M.I.

Firm's name and address (or preparer's, if self-employed)

Firm name

Number and street (Include apt. no.)

City   State   ZIP code

96. Employer identification number (EIN)

97. Preparer's social security number

Certification:
All of the information on this form and in Section I, if completed, is true and complete to the best of my knowledge.

98. Preparer's signature   **Date**

──────────── *ATTENTION* ────────────

If you are filling out the **GRAY and WHITE areas**, go to Instructions, page 8, and complete **WORKSHEET A**. This will tell you whether you must fill out Section I. If you meet certain tax filing and income conditions, you may skip Section I.

If you are filling out the **BLUE and WHITE areas**, go to Instructions, page 8, and complete **WORKSHEET B**. This will tell you whether you must fill out Section I. If you meet certain tax filing and income conditions, you may skip Section I.

Section I: Asset Information

	STUDENT (& SPOUSE)		PARENTS	
			106. Age of your older parent	3 9
Cash, savings, and checking accounts	**99.** $ 500 .00		**107.** $ 2,800 .00	
Other real estate and investments value *(Don't include the home.)*	**100.** $ 0 .00		**108.** $ 83,500 .00	
Other real estate and investments debt *(Don't include the home.)*	**101.** $ 0 .00		**109.** $ .00	
Business value	**102.** $ 0 .00		**110.** $ .00	
Business debt	**103.** $ 0 .00		**111.** $ .00	
Farm value *(See Instructions, pages 8 & 9.)*	**104.** $ 0 .00		**112.** $ .00	
Farm debt *(See Instructions, pages 8 & 9.)*	**105.** $ 0 .00		**113.** $ .00	

MAKE SURE THAT YOU HAVE COMPLETED, DATED, AND SIGNED THE APPLICATION.
Mail the application to: Federal Student Aid Programs, P.O. Box 4016, Iowa City, IA 52243-4016.

Melissa Threeby
CSS No. 3456789
333-33-3333

Financial Aid *P*ROFILE — 1996-97

Complete all sections of the PROFILE Form except Section E. Be certain that everyone giving information on the form signs it.

Section A — Student's Information

1. How many family members will the student (and spouse) support in 1996-97? List their names and give information about them in M. See instructions. |0|

2. Of the number in 1, how many will be in college at least half-time for at least one term in 1996-97? Include yourself. |0,0|

3. What is the student's state of legal residence? |O,R|

4. What is the student's citizenship status?

a. 1 ☒ U.S. citizen
2 ☐ Permanent resident
3 ☐ Neither of the above (Answer "b" and "c" below.)

b. Country of citizenship?

c. Visa classification?

1 ☐ F1   2 ☐ F2   3 ☐ J1   4 ☐ J2   5 ☐ Other

Section B — Student's 1995 Income & Benefits

Don't report parents' information on this page. If married, include spouse's information in Sections B, C, D, and E.

5. The following 1995 U.S. Income tax return figures are (Mark only one box.)

1 ☒ estimated. Will file IRS Form 1040EZ or 1040A. Go to 6.
2 ☐ estimated. Will file IRS Form 1040. Go to 6.
3 ☐ from a completed IRS Form 1040EZ or 1040A. Go to 6.
4 ☐ from a completed IRS Form 1040. Go to 6.
5 ☐ a tax return will not be filed. Skip to 10.

Tax Filers Only

6. 1995 total number of exemptions (IRS Form 1040, line 6e or 1040A, line 6e or 1040EZ — see instructions)   **6.** |0,0|

7. 1995 Adjusted Gross Income from IRS Form 1040, line 31 or 1040A, line 13 or 1040EZ, line 3 (Use the worksheet in the instructions.)   **7.** $ 2,677 .00

8. 1995 U.S. income tax paid (IRS Form 1040, line 47 or 1040A, line 22 or 1040EZ, line 9)   **8.** $ 0 .00

9. 1995 itemized deductions (IRS Form 1040, Schedule A, line 26. Write in "0" if deductions were not itemized.)   **9.** $ 0 .00

10. 1995 income earned from work by student (See instructions.)   **10.** $ 2,677 .00

11. 1995 income earned from work by student's spouse   **11.** $ 0 .00

12. 1995 dividend and interest income   **12.** $ 0 .00

13. 1995 untaxed income and benefits (Give total amount for the year.)

a. Social security benefits (See instructions.)   **13. a.** $ 0 .00

b. Aid to Families with Dependent Children   **b.** $ 0 .00

c. Child support received for all the student's children   **c.** $ 0 .00

d. Earned Income Credit (IRS Form 1040, line 56 or 1040A, line 28c)   **d.** $ 0 .00

e. Other – write total from worksheet, page X.   **e.** $ 0 .00

14. 1995 earnings from Federal Work-Study or other need-based work programs plus any grant and scholarship aid in excess of tuition, fees, books, and supplies   **14.** $ 0 .00

Section C — Student's Assets

15. Cash, savings, and checking accounts $ 500 .00

	What is it worth today?	What is owed on it?
16. Investments (Including Uniform Gifts to Minors. See instructions.)	$ 0 .00	$ .00
17. Home (Renters write in "0.")	$ 0 .00	$ .00
18. Other real estate	$ 0 .00	$ .00
19. Business and farm	$ 0 .00	$ .00

20. If the farm is included in 19, is the student living on the farm?   Yes ☐ 1   No ☐ 2

21. If student owns home, give

a. year purchased |1,9, | b. purchase price $ .00

Section D — Student's Trust Information

22. a. Total value of all trust(s) $ 0 .00

b. Is any income or part of the principal currently available?   Yes ☐ 1   No ☐ 2

c. Who established the trust(s)?

1 ☐ Student's parents   2 ☐ Other

Section E — Student's Expenses

23. 1995 child support paid by student $ 0 .00

24. 1995 medical and dental expenses not covered by insurance (See instructions.) $ 0 .00

Section F — Student's Expected Summer/School-Year Resources for 1996-97

	Amount per month	Number of months
25. Student's veterans benefits (July 1, 1996 – June 30, 1997)	$ 0 .00	

26. Student's (and spouse's) resources (Don't enter monthly amounts.)	Summer 1996 (3 months)	School Year 1996-97 (9 months)
a. Student's wages, salaries, tips, etc.	$ 2,000 .00	$ 0 .00
b. Spouse's wages, salaries, tips, etc.	$ .00	$ 0 .00
c. Other taxable income	$ .00	$ 0 .00
d. Untaxed income and benefits	$ .00	$ 0 .00
e. Grants, scholarships, fellowships, etc. from other than the colleges to which the student is applying (List sources in Section P.)		$ 0 .00
f. Tuition benefits from the parents' and/or the student's or spouse's employer		$ 0 .00
g. Contributions from the student's parent(s)		$ 0 .00
h. Contributions from other relatives, spouse's parents, and all other sources		$ 0 .00

Section G — Parents' Household Information – See page X of the instruction booklet.

27. How many family members will your parents support in 1996-97? Always include yourself (the student). List their names and give information about them in M. `0 4`

28. Of the number in 27, how many will be in college at least half-time for at least one term in 1996-97? Include the student. `1`

29. How many parents will be in college at least half-time in 1996-97? (Mark only one box.)
1 ☒ Neither parent   2 ☐ One parent   3 ☐ Both parents

30. What is the current marital status of your parents? (Mark only one box.)
1 ☐ single   3 ☐ separated   5 ☐ widowed
2 ☒ married   4 ☐ divorced

31. What is your parents' state of legal residence? `O R`

Section H — Parents' Expenses

	1995	Expected 1996
32. Child support paid by the parent(s) completing this form	32 a. $ 0 .00	32. b. $ 0 .00
33. Repayment of educational loans (See instructions.)	33 a. $ 0 .00	33. b. $ 0 .00
34. Medical and dental expenses not covered by insurance (See instructions.)	34 a. $ 0 .00	34. b. $ 0 .00
35. Total elementary, junior high school, and high school tuition paid for dependent children		
Amount paid (Don't include tuition paid for the student.)	35 a. $ 0 .00	35c. $ 0 .00
For how many dependent children? (Don't include the student.)	b. ☐	d. ☐

Section I — Parents' Assets – If parents own all or part of a business or farm, write in its name and the percent of ownership in Section P.

36. Cash, savings, and checking accounts $ 2,800 .00

37. Monthly home mortgage or rental payment (If none, explain in Section P.) $ .00

	What is it worth today?	What is owed on it?
38. Investments	$ 83,500 .00	$ 0 .00
39a. Home (Renters write in "0.")	$ 180,000 .00	$ 154,000 .00

b. year purchased `1 9 9 1`   c. purchase price $ 175,000 .00

	What is it worth today?	What is owed on it?
40. Business	$ .00	$ .00
41. a. Farm	$ .00	$ .00

b. Does family live on the farm?
Yes ☐ 1   No ☐ 2

42. a. Other real estate $ 0 .00 $ .00

b. year purchased `1 9`   c. purchase price $ .00

*P*ROFILE — 1996-97

Section J — Parents' 1994 Income and Benefits

43. 1994 Adjusted Gross Income (IRS Form 1040, line 31 or 1040A, line 13 or 1040EZ, line 3) $ 95,723 .00

44. 1994 U.S. Income tax paid (IRS Form 1040, line 47, 1040A, line 22 or 1040EZ, line 9) $ 17,417 .00

45. 1994 itemized deductions (IRS Form 1040, Schedule A, line 26. Write "0" if deductions were not itemized) $ 6,954 .00

46. 1994 untaxed income and benefits (Include the same types of income & benefits that are listed in 53 a – k.) $ 0 .00

Section K — Parents' 1995 Income & Benefits

47. The following 1995 U.S. income tax return figures are (Mark only one box.)

1 ☐ estimated. Will file IRS Form 1040EZ or 1040A. Go to 48.
2 ☑ estimated. Will file IRS Form 1040. Go to 48.
3 ☐ from a completed IRS Form 1040EZ or 1040A. Go to 48.
4 ☐ from a completed IRS Form 1040. Go to 48.
5 ☐ a tax return will not be filed. Skip to 52.

Tax Filers Only

48. 1995 total number of exemptions (IRS Form 1040, line 6e or 1040A, line 6e or 1040EZ)   **48.** |0|4|

49. 1995 Adjusted Gross Income (IRS Form 1040, line 31 or 1040A, line 13 or 1040EZ, line 3)   **49.** $ 101,581 .00

Breakdown of income in 49

a. Wages, salaries, tips (IRS Form 1040, line 7 or 1040A, line 7 or 1040EZ, line 1)   **49 a.** $100,923 .00

b. Interest income (IRS Form 1040, line 8a or 1040A, line 8a or 1040EZ, line 2)   **b.** $ 658 .00

c. Dividend income (IRS Form 1040, line 9 or 1040A, line 9)   **c.** $ 0 .00

d. Net income (or loss) from business, farm, rents, royalties, partnerships, estates, trusts, etc. (IRS Form 1040, lines 12, 18, and 19) If a loss, enter the amount in (parentheses).   **d.** $ 0 .00

e. Other taxable income such as alimony received, capital gains (or losses), pensions, annuities, etc. (IRS Form 1040, lines 10, 11, 13-15, 16b, 17b, 20, 21b, and 22 or 1040A, line 10)   **e.** $ 0 .00

f. Adjustments to income (IRS Form 1040, line 30 or 1040A, line 12c)   **f.** $ 0 .00

50. 1995 U.S. income tax paid (IRS Form 1040, line 47, 1040A, line 22 or 1040EZ, line 9)   **50.** $ 19,837 .00

51. 1995 itemized deductions (IRS Form 1040, Schedule A, line 26. Write in "0" if deductions were not itemized.)   **51.** $ 7,017 .00

52. 1995 Income earned from work by father   **52.** $ 67,805 .00

53. 1995 Income earned from work by mother   **53.** $ 33,118 .00

54. 1995 untaxed income and benefits (Give total amount for the year. Do not give monthly amounts.)

a. Social security benefits   **54a.** $ 0 .00

b. Aid to Families with Dependent Children   **b.** $ 0 .00

c. Child support received for all children   **c.** $ 0 .00

d. Deductible IRA and/or Keogh payments (See instructions.)   **d.** $ 0 .00

e. Payments to tax-deferred pension and savings plans (See instructions.)   **e.** $ 0 .00

f. Amounts withheld from wages for dependent care and medical spending accounts   **f.** $ 0 .00

g. Earned Income Credit (IRS Form 1040, line 56 or 1040A, line 28c)   **g.** $ 0 .00

h. Housing, food and other living allowances (See instructions.)   **h.** $ 0 .00

i. Tax-exempt interest income (IRS Form 1040, line 8b or 1040A, line 8b)   **i.** $ 0 .00

j. Foreign income exclusion (IRS Form 2555, line 43)   **j.** $ 0 .00

k. Other – write in the total from the worksheet in the instructions, page X.   **k.** $ 0 .00

WRITE ONLY IN THE ANSWER SPACES. DO NOT WRITE ANYWHERE ELSE.

Section L — Parents' 1996 Expected Income & Benefits
(If the expected total income and benefits will differ from the 1995 total income and benefits by $3,000 or more, explain in P.)

55. 1996 income earned from work by father $ 70,000 .00   **57.** 1996 other taxable income $ 1,200 .00

56. 1996 income earned from work by mother $ 35,000 .00   **58.** 1996 untaxed income and benefits $ .00

Section M — Family Member Listing – Give information for all family members but don't give information about yourself. List up to seven other family members here. If there are more than seven, list first those who will be in college at least half-time. List the others in Section P.

59.

	Full name of family member	Age	Claimed as tax exemption in 1995? Yes? No?	Use codes from below.	1995-96 school year				1996-97 school year		
	You — the student applicant				Name of school or college	Year in school	Scholarships and grants	Parents' contri-bution	Attend college at least one term full-time half-time		Name of school or college
2	John Threeby	39	☒ ☐	1					1☐ 2☐		
3	Maria Threeby	36	☒ ☐	1					1☐ 2☐		
4	Daniel Threeby	15	☒ ☐	3					1☐ 2☐		
5			☐ ☐						1☐ 2☐		
6			☐ ☐						1☐ 2☐		
7			☐ ☐						1☐ 2☐		
8			☐ ☐						1☐ 2☐		

Write in the correct code from the right. ↑   1 = Student's parent   3 = Student's brother or sister   5 = Student's son or daughter   7 = Other
2 = Student's stepparent   4 = Student's husband or wife   6 = Student's grandparent

Section N — Parents' Information

60. Mark one: ☒ Father ☐ Stepfather ☐ Legal guardian ☐ Other (Explain in P.)

a. Name John Threeby   Age 3 9

b. Mark if: ☐ Self-employed ☐ Unemployed – Date last employed: _____

c. Occupation Sales Manager

d. Employer Thirdburg Dodge   No. years 8

e. Work telephone (optional) ☐☐☐ - ☐☐☐ - ☐☐☐☐

f. Retirement plans: ☒ Social security ☒ Union/employer ☐ Civil service/state ☐ IRA/Keogh/tax-deferred ☐ Military ☐ Other

61. Mark one: ☒ Mother ☐ Stepmother ☐ Legal guardian ☐ Other (Explain in P.)

a. Name Maria Threeby   Age 3 6

b. Mark if: ☐ Self-employed ☐ Unemployed – Date last employed: _____

c. Occupation Real Estate Sales

d. Employer Third Best Homes   No. years 7

e. Work telephone (optional) ☐☐☐ - ☐☐☐ - ☐☐☐☐

f. Retirement plans: ☒ Social security only ☐ Union/employer ☐ Civil service/state ☐ IRA/Keogh/tax-deferred ☐ Military ☐ Other

Section O — Divorced, Separated, or Remarried Parents

(To be answered by the parent who completes this form, if the student's natural or adoptive parents are divorced, separated, or remarried.)

62. a. Year of separation ☐☐   Year of divorce ☐☐

b. Other parent's name _____

Home address _____

_____

Occupation/Employer _____

c. According to court order, when will support for the student end? ☐☐ ☐☐ Month Year

d. Who last claimed the student as a tax exemption? _____

_____ Year? ☐☐

e. How much does the other parent plan to contribute to the student's education for the 1995-96 school year? $_____ .00

f. Is there an agreement specifying this contribution for the student's education? Yes ☐ No ☐

Section P — Explanations/Special Circumstances

Use this space to explain any unusual expenses such as high medical or dental expenses, educational and other debts, child care, elder care, or special circumstances. Also, give information for any outside scholarships you have been awarded.

Certification:

All the information on this form is true and complete to the best of my knowledge. If asked, I agree to give proof of the information that I have given on this form. I realize that this proof may include a copy of my U.S., state, or local income tax returns. I certify that all information is correct at this time, and that I will send timely notice of any significant change in family income or assets, financial situation, college plans of other children, or the receipt of other scholarships or grants.

1 _____ Student's signature

2 _____ Student's spouse's signature

3 _____ Father's (stepfather's) signature

4 _____ Mother's (stepmother's) signature

Date this form was completed:
☐☐ ☐☐   1☐ 1995
Month Day   2☐ 1996
  3☐ 1997
  Year

The Threebys bought their current home in 1991 for $175,000. In a stagnant market, its value has grown to just $180,000. Their mortgage balance is $154,000 on which they're paying $1,180 a month. Their home equity is $26,000.

Melissa, too, was careful about accurately reporting all of these numbers on her FAFSA and PROFILE. Let's look at the FAFSA worksheet to see what they do for her.

MELISSA'S MAGIC NUMBER

Melissa's parents had a total income last year of $101,581. They paid federal taxes of $19,837. Again both of these numbers are taken right off of their tax return.

As Oregon residents, the Threebys can take 9 percent ($9,142) of their income (Table 1) for other taxes. Their Social Security taxes come to $7,088. Like the Twofers, they are a family of four with one college student, so they can protect $16,670 (Table 4) of their income. And they get the maximum $2,500 employment allowance.

Allowances for the Threeby parents add up to $55,237. Subtracting that from their income leaves $46,344 "available" for college.

John and Maria's assets are $83,500 in investments plus $2,800 in checking. That's $86,300. As the older parent at age 39 (Table 6), John can protect $30,100 of his assets. That leaves $56,200 available as Discretionary Net Worth. And 12 percent of DNW is $6,744.

Add the Threebys' $46,344 from income and $6,744 from assets. You have $53,088. Apply the final step (Table 7) and you learn they're expected to spend $21,044 of it on Melissa's freshman year.

Now for Melissa's share. Her income was $2,677. She gets the $1,750 automatic deduction for dependent students, a $205 allowance for Social Security taxes, and $160 (Table 1) for other taxes. Her allowance total is $2,115. She has $562 left as income "available" for college.

Melissa's expected contribution is half her available income, or $281, plus 35 percent of her assets (the $500 in her checking account) or $175. That totals $456. A parental contribution of $21,044 plus a student contribution of $456 produces a nice round EFC of $21,500. It's high but, as we'll see, not high enough at some places to deny her financial aid.

THE OTHER MAGIC NUMBERS

Congratulations! You have just gone through the process that the financial aid folks call Need Analysis. And you've done it three times.

Now you're almost through the process. You have Expected Family Contributions for Jennifer, Michael, and Melissa based on their FAFSA information. Those EFCs, devised from a formula based on federal law, will determine their eligibility for government aid programs at all colleges.

But they also filled out the PROFILE because four of the five colleges (all but Cottey) want it. Each school will use information on the PROFILE in its own way to come up with an EFC for awarding its own money in the form of tuition discounts, which often is the bulk of a student's package.

Perhaps you think Michael Twofer gets a break because his parents split. He does in the federal programs. But three colleges, Notre Dame, Gettysburg, and William & Mary, sent Michael a third form— the Divorced/Separated Parent's Statement. They asked him to have his Dad fill it out and send it in. Then they looked seriously at his father's income in building Michael's aid package.

At William & Mary, which figures EFC the federal way but uses PROFILE information to supplement it, Jennifer got a break. Aid Director Ed Irish used her estimated summer income of $2,000, reported on the PROFILE, instead of last year's $6,762 earnings. It slashed her EFC nicely. Says Irish: "She obviously worked hard during high school. We don't expect her to earn that kind of income working here."

There's no formula to tell you precisely what your Need will be when a college calculates it. The worksheet in Chapter Two will get you in the ball park. But each school reviews the numbers and the results can vary. Some aid directors, in moments of candor, admit they often adjust the numbers based on a "feel" of what a student can pay. Says Notre Dame's Joe Russo: "It's not a perfect science, but rather an attempt to get a rough gauge of the family's ability to contribute."

In most cases, the student's share of the Expected Family Contribution will be higher when a college figures it. They don't allow the $1,750 automatic deduction from students' income. And most colleges will require a minimum student contribution, often $900 for incoming freshmen. The parents' share, as you will see, occasionally can be lower in the college calculations than in the federal formula, even with home equity in the equation.

Our students, as it turns out, each have three EFCs that were used to build their aid packages. One is from the federal formula, the others were calculated independently by Notre Dame and Gettysburg. North Carolina and William & Mary supplement the federal EFC with information from the PROFILE. Cottey awards all aid from the federal EFC.

Before we look at our students' packages, let's compare their EFCs. Then we'll subtract the EFCs from the costs of their five colleges and learn their Need—their magic numbers. (See page 111.)

You'll notice the Cost of Attendance differs for students at some schools. They allow a transportation expense based on the student's distance from campus. At Notre Dame, for example, it will cost Michael less to travel from Ohio than Jennifer from Virginia or Melissa from Oregon. Other schools figure a flat sum for travel, books, and miscellaneous expenses. At Gettysburg, it's $1,000.

At William & Mary, Jennifer's cost is lower because she lives in Virginia. And her federal EFC is lower than at other schools because it was calculated on her summer anticipated income, not last year's income.

EFC	Federal	Notre Dame	Gettysburg
For Jennifer			
Parent contribution	5,547	3,310	6,645
Student contribution	+ 3,643	+ 4,880	+ 4,610
Expected Family Cont.	9,190	8,190	11,255
For Michael			
Parent contribution	803	17,470	5,805
Student contribution	+ 0	+ 1,230	+ 930
Expected Family Cont.	803	18,700	6,735
For Melissa			
Parent contribution	21,044	16,750	21,770
Student contribution	+ 456	+ 1,375	+ 1,375
Expected Family Cont.	21,500	18,125	23,145

And their Needs	Jennifer	Michael	Melissa
Cottey cost	11,100	11,050	11,200
EFC (federal)	– 9,190	– 803	– 21,500
Cottey Need	1,910	10,247	0
Gettysburg cost	25,380	25,380	25,380
EFC (school)	– 11,255	– 6,735	– 23,145
Gettysburg Need	14,125	18,645	2,235
Notre Dame cost	24,530	23,440	24,530
EFC (school)	– 8,190	– 18,700	– 18,125
Notre Dame Need	16,340	4,740	6,405
North Carolina cost	14,950	14,950	14,950
EFC (federal)	– 9,190	– 803	– 21,500
North Carolina Need	5,760	14,147	0
William & Mary cost	10,682	19,594	19,594
EFC (federal)	– 3,060	– 803	– 21,500
William & Mary Need	7,622	18,791	0

Now let's move to the five campuses where financial aid officials have our students' applications on their desks. It's time to decide just what those magic numbers will produce.

JENNIFER'S AID PACKAGE

Here's what Jennifer's award letter offers her:

	Cottey	Gettys	ND	UNC	W&M
Cost	11,100	25,380	24,530	14,950	10,682
Work-Study		900	2,000	800	950
Perkins Loan		2,700	2,460		1,000
Stafford Loan	910	2,625	2,625		2,625
College Grant	1,000	10,600	9,000	2,500	3,000
Total Aid	1,910	14,125	16,325	5,760	7,575

At first glance, it looks like Notre Dame has the best deal. Its package is $2,200 better than any other school's offer. At second glance, when Jennifer compares aid packages to the schools' costs, William & Mary clearly shines. Jennifer and her parents must come up with about $3,100 for a year at Williamsburg, $8,000 at South Bend, roughly $9,000 at North Carolina or Cottey and $11,000 to go to Gettysburg. Gettysburg's $14,125 may seem much more generous than the $1,900 from Cottey or $5,760 from North Carolina, but it leaves more out-of-pocket costs for the Oneder family. (If Jennifer lived in North Carolina, her Need at Chapel Hill would be zero and she would get no aid. Her EFC is higher than the $7,400 cost for North Carolina residents.)

Most of the numbers are not a surprise. When Jennifer calculated her EFC on the worksheet, after filling out her FAFSA, she thought her family contribution would be in the $9,000 range. When she figured it from the PROFILE, including home equity, it was over $11,000. Indeed, Jennifer thinks the offers from Notre Dame and William & Mary—which leave her with less than $9,000 to pay— are surprisingly good.

But look again, more closely. The Notre Dame package includes $5,300 in loans which eventually must be repaid. William & Mary asks her to borrow more than $3,600. They are the only packages that include two loans; the other schools suggest just one. At Notre Dame, $2,000 of Jennifer's aid comes from a campus job. Three schools propose she earn less than $1,000 by working. Notre Dame's campus job might pay higher hourly wages than the other schools; Jennifer could find out by calling its financial aid office.

Now look at Cottey. Its financial aid folks tell Jennifer she can come to their pastoral campus in rural Missouri by borrowing a mere $910. And a job is not part of the deal.

In Firstville, Virginia, Jennifer's father the math teacher gets out his calculator for some serious button-pushing. He has one of those books showing loan payment schedules that he bought for $3.98 at an office supply store. He learns—figuring a Perkins Loan at 5 percent interest, a Stafford at 6.22—that if Jennifer takes Notre Dame's offer she'll pay $1,591 interest on that debt after she leaves college. And that's just for her first year.

In William & Mary's package, the interest would be $1,128; at Gettysburg, $855; at Chapel Hill, $654; at Cottey, $280. Of course, if a loan is repaid faster than the allotted 10 years, the interest is less.

For the Oneder family, Notre Dame now becomes $600 more expensive than Cottey over the long haul and about the same price as Chapel Hill. At William & Mary, that $3,100 cost to the family on the award letter has become $4,200.

Jennifer will weigh many other factors besides money in deciding which college to attend. But when money is considered, she and her parents will look at the loans she must obtain and the long-range cost of repaying them.

WHY JENNIFER GOT IT

Go back and look at Jennifer's EFCs as figured by the government formula and by the two private colleges. As expected, her own share is higher at Notre Dame and Gettysburg because they threw out the $1,750 deduction from her income that the federal formula automatically allows.

But her parents' contribution expected by Notre Dame is less than the federal formula. At Gettysburg it's considerably higher. Gettysburg looked at the Oneders' $54,000 home equity and their investment assets and decided they could pay $6,600 this year for Jennifer. Notre Dame looked at their relatively low annual income and decided they should pay just $3,600.

Neither we nor Jennifer will know precisely how those numbers were obtained. Russo and his counterpart, Ron Shunk, at Gettysburg, say only that they closely follow the College Board formula (Chapter Two) in their own review. "If requested by the family, explanations would be provided," Russo explains.

Remember "professional judgment," that all-important term described in Chapter Six. Russo, Shunk, and aid directors at almost all selective schools in their price range apply professional judgment on a student-by-student basis.

William & Mary's Ed Irish used professional judgment when he saw Jennifer's $6,746 income for last year, assumed she wouldn't be earning that much in college, and chopped it to $2,000 for the federal formula.

Says Russo, "Some people see things differently; some don't. There are factors in each case that can be viewed differently by each and every college involved."

North Carolina and Cottey defined Jennifer's EFC as $9,190, the number from the federal formula.

All five schools will say they met Jennifer's need. All five did give her an aid package covering the difference between her EFC and the Cost of Attendance. But Expected Family Contribution, as you are learning, often depends on the eye of the expecter.

If Notre Dame was more generous in its expectations, it was stingier in its award. It's asking Jennifer to borrow twice as much as anyone else proposes. That's due to its philosophy of assembling financial aid packages.

Like most highly selective schools including the Ivy League, Notre Dame starts with what it calls "self-help." The first pieces in its package are loans and jobs. Jennifer was given a maximum Stafford Loan of $2,625, a $2,700 Perkins Loan and a $2,000 Work-Study job. That left $9,000 of Need, which Notre Dame covered with its own money.

At the other schools she heard from, the process was reversed. Gettysburg starts by covering 70 percent of a student's need from its own funds. So it gave Jennifer a $10,600 grant (discount), then added a Stafford Loan and a job to meet the other 30 percent. North Carolina starts by calculating its own EFC, meeting at least half that Need with a college grant, then using loans and jobs to meet the rest of the Need defined by the federal formula.

HOW JENNIFER COULD DO BETTER

Jennifer's $9,190 federal Expected Family Contribution, and the others figured by the colleges, could have been significantly lower. Some planning and knowing the rules a few years back would have helped.

Oliver and Olivia Oneder are diligent savers. Some of their money was put away to pay their two kids' college bills but much of it is for retirement. But they don't have an IRA. The only IRA money that must be reported on the FAFSA is the contribution from last year's income. Amounts from years past can be ignored. If the Oneders opened an IRA 11 years ago, depositing $2,500 a year, it would have grown to about $50,000. Only the $2,500 they put in last year would be considered in the income stream on the FAFSA, leaving $47,500 unreported.

Their Discretionary Net Worth would drop from $88,831 to $41,331. Their expected contributions for Jennifer and her brother would drop from $5,547 to $4,207. Jennifer's federal EFC would drop from $9,190 to $7,850.

Then there's Grandma. It was nice of her to give Jennifer that $200 annual birthday gift. It would have been even nicer if she just told Jennifer about it but kept the money in her own name. Then

Jennifer's assets would be just the $450 in her checking account. Her student contribution would drop from $3,643 to $2,033. Her EFC would be down to $6,240.

If Grandma was reluctant to keep the money, she would have been better advised to give it to Oliver and Olivia instead of Jennifer. To figure the EFC, the formula takes 12 percent of parents' unprotected assets, 35 percent of the student's.

The Oneders also can use the "Mom Goes to College" tactic. It's a perfectly legal way to slash the federal EFC but it's also likely to be disallowed by the Notre Dames, Gettysburgs, and North Carolinas in their own calculations, if they spot it.

Remember one of the final steps in the formula: The parental contribution is divided by the number of family members in college. For federal aid, the law defines a college student as anyone taking at least six credits.

Olivia Oneder, who works part time, always wanted to take a couple of classes to improve her communications and computer skills. Now is the right time. If she enrolls at Firstville State for two three-credit courses, she's a college student. The Oneder's family contribution is now divided by three, not two. Jennifer's EFC— already reduced by the steps described above —would fall to $4,838, just over half its original level.

Now, everything else being equal, Jennifer likely would get aid packages totaling about $20,000 from Gettysburg and Notre Dame, $10,000 from North Carolina, $6,000 from Cottey.

And Jennifer can make the packages even better by what she does at Firstville High. We've said it before and it's time to say it again: The more attractive a student is to a college, the more generous the college will usually be to the student.

The better students get, in financial aid folks' jargon, "preferential packaging." It means different things on different campuses. To Eleanor Morris, aid director at Chapel Hill, it could mean more money, a more attractive package, or both. To Shunk at Gettysburg, who says he gives every student all he or she deserves, it means a better ratio of grants to loans. To Ed Irish at William & Mary, it means which of several packages a student receives.

At North Carolina, Morris says the 100 best students—who have a financial Need—of the 3,300 in each freshman class get preferential packaging. If Jennifer were among those exceptional students, she would receive her entire $5,760 as a grant from the college. No loans to be repaid. No jobs to perform.

At Gettysburg, Shunk looks at better offers for students with SAT scores over 1300 and in the top ten percent of their high school classes. They can get Gettysburg grants of up to $10,000—without regard to their magic number—and better grant-to-loan packages to meet their Need. If Jennifer has those credentials, her cost at Gettysburg is slashed to $1,000 and she could borrow all of it.

At William & Mary, Jennifer's academic record earns the second-best package of grants and loans. If she had done a little better in school, her W&M grant would be $1,000 higher; and she would not have been offered a Work-Study job. W&M's Irish says the top 10 to 15 percent of each freshman class get the better package.

MICHAEL'S AID PACKAGE

Michael Twofer, with a much different set of financial circumstances, would do even better with an exceptional high school record. Let's see how he fares:

	Cottey	Gettys	ND	UNC	W&M
Cost	11,050	25,380	23,440	14,950	19,594
Pell Grant	1,450	1,450	1,450	1,450	1,450
SEOG	400	2,000		700	
Work-Study	1,300	1,300	2,000	1,500	1,200
Perkins Loan		2,700	3,000		1,000
Stafford Loan	2,625	2,625	2,625	2,625	2,625
College Grant	3,022	11,300		1,800	5,000
Total Aid	8,797	18,675	8,775	11,075	11,275

When he opens the award letters, Michael says: "Wow! Eighteen grand from Gettysburg." Then he remembers Gettysburg costs $25,000. He and his mother would have to find a quick $7,000. His face falls farther when he reads the word from Notre Dame. It offers $8,775 toward an annual bill of $23,440. No way, at all, he thinks.

William & Mary gives him $11,275 but its cost for non-Virginians is $19,594. North Carolina's package of $11,075 requires Michael to borrow $5,625 in two loans, then come up with another $3,875 to meet the $14,950 out-of-state cost. Better but still not good.

The best offer clearly comes from Cottey (where Michael would have to be Michelle; it's a women's college). Its aid package is just $2,200 short of its cost and it asks Michael to borrow only $2,625 in a Stafford Loan.

When Michael calculated his federal EFC from the FAFSA worksheet, he was elated at the prospect of attending college for an expenditure of just $803. His mother, even on a nurse's pay, could handle that.

But he suspected it might not happen when he got those letters from Notre Dame, Gettysburg, and William & Mary asking for his father's financial information. Dad didn't like it but he sent in the forms, still insisting that his financial obligation to Michael ended at age 18.

Now Michael reads the award letters and thinks he won't be attending any of these colleges for $803. But wait! Maybe he will. Down at the bottom of the letters is something about Unsubsidized Stafford Loans and PLUS Loans, not based on need and not included in the aid packages.

Michael studies the rules. Unsubsidized Stafford Loans are available to any student. But his aid packages, from all four schools, include a $2,625 Subsidized Stafford and that's the most a freshman can borrow in the Stafford program. PLUS looks more promising. A parent can borrow the difference between a school's aid package and Cost of Attendance. Perhaps Mom could borrow the $2,200 he needs to go to Cottey or the $3,875 to get to Chapel Hill.

Perhaps. But the prospect should be carefully studied. Repayment of PLUS loans, unlike the Stafford and Perkins, is not deferred until the student leaves school. Mom must start making payments in 60 days. Perhaps a better course would be for Mom to talk to Dad.

WHY MICHAEL GOT IT

Dad is the source of some of Michael's aid and the cause of many of his problems.

Michael's FAFSA produced a very low EFC, $803, because his parents are divorced and his mother is not financially well off. That EFC automatically qualifies him for a Pell Grant of $1,450, the first item in all his aid packages. It makes him eligible for a SEOG, at each school's discretion. Gettysburg gave him a $2,000 SEOG; two other schools made it smaller.

When Notre Dame and Gettysburg calculated their own EFCs, they looked at Dr. Thomas Twofer's circumstances. They saw an $83,000 annual income and $90,000 in assets. They saw a second marriage that has produced no children. They decided some of Thomas' resources should be available to help Michael.

When William & Mary looked at Dad's situation, it decided he should continue to contribute the $3,600 he has been paying for child support, his divorce agreement notwithstanding. "We normally don't ask for a divorced parent's statement," says W&M's Irish. "But when we see a doctor or a lawyer, we will."

Go back to the comparison of Michael's EFCs. Notre Dame was especially rigorous. It asks for a $17,470 family contribution, almost all of which would have to come from Dad. Gettysburg put it at $5,805, still $5,000 higher than figured by the federal formula. If Dad resists, Michael won't be going to Gettysburg or South Bend.

Notice the wide disparity in colleges' grants to Michael from their own money: $11,300 from Gettysburg, nothing from Notre Dame. Again it reflects two opposite philosophies. Notre Dame met Michael's Need entirely with "self-help" plus the Pell Grant for which he automatically qualified. Gettysburg started with the Pell, met 70 percent of Michael's Need from its own money, then added self-help.

Notice, too, the difference in Michael's share of his EFC. It's zero in the federal formula because he earned less than $1,750. But most schools using the PROFILE, like Gettysburg, ask for at least $900 from every student regardless of his or her finances. Notre Dame asks for $1,200.

HOW MICHAEL COULD DO BETTER

He could start by moving in with his aunt in Charlotte, N.C., and staying long enough to become a legal resident of the state. Not only would the cost of UNC–Chapel Hill be halved, he would get enough aid to cover it.

But he wouldn't do so well at William & Mary even as a Virginia resident. Remember, W&M figured Michael's need the federal way, then decided Daddy should contribute $3,200.

The financial aid folks at Chapel Hill and William & Mary calculated alternate packages for Michael if he were a North Carolina or Virginia resident. Here's how they look:

	In-State	Out-of-State
UNC–Chapel Hill		
Cost	7,400	14,950
Pell Grant	1,450	1,450
SEOG	300	700
Work-Study	800	1,500
Perkins Loan	2,660	3,000
Stafford Loan		2,625
College Grant	1,380	1,800
Total Aid	6,590	11,075
William & Mary		
Cost	10,682	19,594
Pell Grant	1,450	1,450
Work-Study	0	1,200
Perkins Loan	550	1,000
Stafford Loan	2,625	2,625
College Grant	900	5,000
Total Aid	5,525	11,275

Guess what: The total aid package for Michael as a North Carolina resident is $810 less than the cost of UNC–Chapel Hill. That's as close to $803 as he will get.

North Carolina's Morris says she just doesn't have enough money to meet Michael's Need as an out-of-stater, even when doubling the numbers in discretionary programs such as SEOG and Work-Study. Much of the school's own money, she says, comes from donors who restrict its use to North Carolina residents.

As a nonresident, Michael is "gapped." His Need is not fully met. As a North Carolinian, he gets a year at Chapel Hill for $810 of his Mom's money and a $2,660 paid-after-he-graduates loan.

There's not much Michael can do to lower his federal EFC, as Jennifer Oneder did, because it can't go much lower. Two courses at college for his mother would cut the EFC by $400 but they might cost her that much or more.

At Notre Dame, Joe Russo suggests a way Michael can lower his Notre Dame EFC. He can appeal. Russo considers Michael's $803 federal EFC an "artificial need," because it ignores his wealthy father.

Like every other student, Michael also can help himself in high school. If he were among the top 100 students entering Chapel Hill, even coming from Secondtown, Ohio, his full $14,950 Need would be met—all but $2,000 in grants. No job would be required.

Now let's look at Melissa and how she does with a high EFC.

MELISSA'S AID PACKAGE

	Cottcy	Gcttys	ND	UNC	W&M
Cost	11,200	25,380	24,530	14,950	19,594
Work-Study			2,000		
Perkins Loan			1,750		
Stafford Loan			2,625		
College Grant		2,200			
Total Aid	0	2,200	6,375	0	0

Melissa saw it coming. When she filled out the FAFSA and calculated that $21,500 EFC, she resigned herself to the realization that her parents would be her principal source of college funds. They can handle it. Together, John and Maria Threeby earned $101,000 last year and have $86,000 in the bank.

Still Melissa, denied aid by two colleges, gets some from the two whose costs are higher than her EFC. Notre Dame's package is clearly most attractive. It offers her an opportunity to borrow $4,325 at low interest with payments postponed until after college. Her father likes that. If that's where Melissa decides to go, it's $4,325 less he must send to Notre Dame that can be working for him in mutual funds.

Gettysburg offers a $2,200 discount, bringing its tab down to $23,180. Notre Dame's package reduces its cost to $18,700. Both costs still are higher than North Carolina and Cottey, which offer no aid at all. If Melissa chooses Gettysburg, the Threebys will pay twice as much as at Cottey. Cost will be a significant factor as Melissa and her parents talk about her decision.

Wherever she goes to college, Melissa's parents need not spend a cent of their savings. They can borrow the whole thing, minus her financial aid, in a PLUS loan at about 7.43 percent interest as of July 1, 1994 (the rate changes every June).

Responding to Melissa, Notre Dame and Gettysburg remain consistent in their fundamentally opposite approaches to aid packaging. Notre Dame offered self-help: two loans and a job. Gettysburg met her entire Need with a discount.

HOW MELISSA GOT IT

Melissa's one substantial package from Notre Dame is a clear example of how the formula used by selective colleges requesting the PROFILE can be better for the student than the federal calculation.

Melissa's federal EFC is $21,500. At Notre Dame, it's $18,125. And the standard formula using PROFILE information puts it even lower, at $17,454. While assessing home equity as part of her income, the PROFILE formula grants higher allowances for "other" taxes and protects a larger percentage of parents' income. That balance favors the Threebys, whose equity is relatively low and income relatively high.

HOW MELISSA COULD DO BETTER

Two tactics recommended for Jennifer Oneder's family also could help Melissa:

If Melissa's father put $2,500 a year into an IRA for the last 11 years instead of into another type of investment, his family's Discretionary Net Worth drops from $56,200 to $28,700. Melissa's federal EFC falls from $21,500 to $18,821.

If Mom or Dad enrolls for six credits at a local college, Melissa's EFC plunges to $10,095. At North Carolina and William & Mary, which use the federal EFC, she would have a Need and be eligible for aid. At Notre Dame, Joe Russo says he would allow Mom's actual costs as a minor adjustment to the family income stream but would not include her in the calculation that divides the expected parental ability to contribute by the number of family members in college.

WHAT HAPPENS NOW?

Jennifer, Michael, and Melissa must decide where they are going to college. The information they received from the financial aid offices will be considered in concert with many other factors— academic offerings, location, campus size, student body makeup, social life—to decide if they'll continue their lives in Indiana, Missouri, North Carolina, Pennsylvania, or Virginia. Each has visited the five campuses to talk with faculty and students and get a feel for his or her comfort level.

When the decision is made, they will sign and return all five award letters, marking "decline" on four. On the offer accepted, each has the option of declining individual pieces of the package, usually by drawing a line through the items rejected.

Melissa, for example, may decide she doesn't want to work at Notre Dame. She'll decline the $2,000 Work-Study offer and accept the loans, at Dad's insistence. Jennifer might decide she can get by at Gettysburg without borrowing or working but she'll take the $10,600 grant.

Be aware, however, that rejecting parts of the package produces different reactions at different schools the next time you apply for money. When Melissa prepares for her sophomore year at Notre Dame and applies again for financial aid, Russo will ask why she didn't need the Work-Study money. If she doesn't have a reasonable answer, it could be a factor in his review of that year's aid decision. When Jennifer applies as a sophomore at Gettysburg, Shunk likely will offer the same package once again, fully expecting her once again to decline the job and loans.

A COMPARISON

Are the financial aid rules fair? The people in Congress who wrote them hope they are. All financial aid directors who ever signed award letters say they try to make them as fair as they can. But as you've seen they frequently are not.

For our three hypothetical students, let's compare their parents' annual income with the total financial aid they were awarded by all five schools:

	Jennifer	Michael	Melissa
Parents' income	$48,835	$112,506	$101,581
Total financial aid	$45,695	$ 58,597	$ 8,575

Michael Twofer's parents earn the most and he got the most aid. The reason, of course, is Michael's parents neither live with each other nor speak to each other. But they're still Michael's parents. And that's one of the stickiest issues currently debated in the financial aid "community."

At USA TODAY's annual Financial Aid Hotline (see Chapter Ten), aid directors sit around an informal luncheon table and the debate spontaneously erupts. Should they go after the noncustodial parent and require him or her to pay her share of his or her daughter's education? Many say yes. Many say no. And they say it with equal vigor.

Michael Twofer's mother is just getting by. If she were a single parent and never married, Michael would deserve all the aid he could get. And that low $803 EFC might get it for him. Michael's father is an affluent physician. If he and Michael's mother were still married, Michael would most likely receive little or no aid.

As it turns out, Michael's EFC ranges from very high to very low and opinions on what he deserves vary just as widely. Is Michael being penalized because his mother once was married or rewarded because she is divorced?

No one, at the moment, has an answer. But we can look at some ways any parent can plan, from the day a child is born, to ease the financial pain of college. We take that look in the next chapter.

CHAPTER EIGHT

MAKING IT EASIER

...a head start, careful planning along the way, helps

Give up a Coke and a bag of chips a day and you can pay for a year at college. USA TODAY's Tamara Henry came up with that calculation based on the price charged by her office vending machine: 55¢ for a soft drink, 45¢ for chips.

The catch: you must start giving up Coke and chips the day your child is born, invest that $1 a day where it will earn 8 percent, and by the time your kid is ready for college you'll have $11,000. That might be enough to pay for one year, perhaps two if he or she picks a low-priced school.

The principle, however, is sound. Put away $4 every working day, $80 a month, and on your child's eighteenth birthday you'll have a $44,000 nest egg. Today, that would buy four years at just about any state university and one third of the nation's private colleges. You would have no need to fill out financial aid forms.

Not many parents have the foresight to start planning that early. A recent *Money* magazine survey showed half of all parents don't save for college and just 25 percent are saving by the time their child is 8 years old.

Regardless of when you begin, putting a fixed sum each month into a college account is a good head start for the day when the bills must be paid. The magic of compounding—reinvesting interest as it's earned—builds a total return on your investment higher than the published interest rate.

Half of today's parents don't put away money for their children's college.

HOW MUCH WILL YOU NEED?

A lot of people are guessing but no one really knows. If a college costs $20,000 this year, it likely will go up to about $21,000 next year, perhaps $22,000 to $22,500 a year later. Beyond that, even the best experts only can guess at the factors influencing cost-setting decisions.

Some experts have produced tables estimating the cost of a four-year college education 20 years into the future. Most of them use a 7 percent inflation rate, figuring the cost of tuition, room, and board will increase 7 percent a year. That's probably high.

You can pretty safely assume college costs will go up a maximum of 7 percent each year.

College costs soared during the 1980s, jumping at the rate of 7 to 10 percent a year, but in the last few years the increases have not been so steep. In the 1993–94 school year, The College Board reports the average cost (tuition, room, and board) at a four-year private college was $15,818, a one-year increase of 5.3 percent. At four-year public schools the average was $6,207, up 6.4 percent.

And 1993–94 was the third consecutive year that the average cost increase was lower than the year before.

There is little indication that annual increases will return to the 7 percent level. Colleges were burned by negative publicity in the late 1980s when their prices were climbing twice as fast as the cost of living. Since then, presidents have been highly sensitive to the headlines any increase will generate. And through the rest of the 1990s, colleges will be in a buyer's market where the number of available spaces will be greater than the number of students applying. Those two pressures will combine to keep cost increases low.

Total financial aid money awarded in 1993–94 was 5 percent more than that of the year before.

As costs increase, so does financial aid. The College Board reports that in 1993–94 aid from all sources—government, colleges, and private organizations—was up 5 percent.

HOW MUCH MUST YOU SAVE?

It depends, of course, on when you start. And as with all planning, the earlier you start the better.

If your child is entering eighth grade you could put away $677 a month and when he graduates from high school have $50,000, enough to cover four years at Flagship State U., even with 7 percent inflation.

If you start in fourth grade, $315 a month will produce the same $50,000 but Flagship State undoubtedly will cost more. If college is just two years away, you'll have to invest $1,925 a month to get $50,000. And those numbers are based on investments earning 8.5 percent total return.

The folks at T. Rowe Price, the mutual fund company, calculated the cost of four years' college for the next 20 years, assuming annual increases of 6 percent. And they figure how much you must save to meet those costs, depending on when you start. Their calculations are on page 129.

Making regular deposits into a savings account or a personal investment plan is the most popular way to prepare for college expenses, but there are other programs to encourage college savings:

- The government offers Series EE savings bonds that guarantee at least 6 percent interest if held five years. The income is tax-free and the risk is zero.

SAVINGS ADDS UP

Here's how much you must save each month, assuming an 8.5 percent total return, to accumulate $50,000:

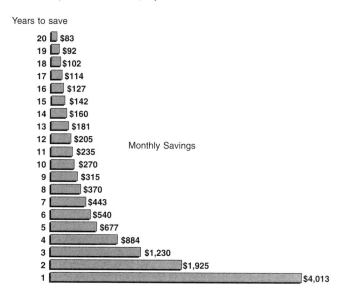

Years to save

20	$83
19	$92
18	$102
17	$114
16	$127
15	$142
14	$160
13	$181
12	$205
11	$235
10	$270
9	$315
8	$370
7	$443
6	$540
5	$677
4	$884
3	$1,230
2	$1,925
1	$4,013

Monthly Savings

Source: USA TODAY research

- The College Savings Bank of Princeton, New Jersey, sells certificates of deposit guaranteed to match increases in college costs. You deposit the current cost of a year at Flagship State and, when college time arrives, you'll receive whatever a year at Flagship costs then. If Flagship's annual increases are 6 percent, that's what your investment will have earned. If you can stand a little more risk, your money would do a lot better elsewhere.
- Some states allow you to pay for college now, locking in today's prices whenever your child is ready to attend. Those plans severely limit your child's choice of colleges—usually to in-state public institutions—and offer a lower return than many other investments.

PROFITABLE JUGGLING ACTS

Careful planning in the years before college can not only build a nest egg of your own funds, it can also help you get more financial aid. If you calculated your magic number on the worksheets back in Chapter Two of this book, you already may have discovered ways to juggle assets for greater profit.

Take a look at how you handle your assets in the years before college; it could mean more aid for you.

The juggling is legal. Just as you might take steps to reduce your income taxes, such as paying off your credit cards with a home equity loan, there are steps you can take to make the financial aid formula work to your advantage. Among them:

- Don't put savings in the student's name. The formula takes a larger bite of the student's assets for the expected family contribution than it does from the parents. And if grandparents are willing, let them keep the college nest egg in their own names. No formula yet has asked about grandparents' assets.
- Discourage gifts of money from generous friends and relatives. If Aunt Julia wants to give a student a $1,000 savings bond for a college nest egg, ask her to keep the money and write the check when it's time to pay tuition. Or put the bond in her own name. If the student owns the bond, the formula counts it. But it doesn't worry about Aunt Julia's bonds.
- If you plan to sell stocks, bonds, or mutual funds for college money, do it before the student's last year in high school. Capital gains earned the year before you apply for financial aid must be reported as income, reducing your magic number.
- Put other family members in college. Mom and Dad each could enroll for six credits at the local community college and be

considered half-time students by the financial aid formula. As I explain elsewhere, your magic number climbs substantially with each family member in college.

- If your family has large medical or dental expenses not covered by insurance, pay them all in the calendar year before you apply for student aid. If you are applying to one of the colleges that wants the PROFILE, the formula will deduct those expenses from your income.
- Put as much as you can into home equity. If your bank permits, pay down the mortgage principal. If you are buying a home, make as large a down payment as you can afford. Home equity is not considered as an asset by the formula that controls all government aid programs.
- Move assets into IRAs and other retirement plans at least a year before you apply. Retirement savings aren't considered when the formula adds up parents' assets.

Many factors other than college must go into a family's financial planning. All of the above suggestions must be considered in the context of taxes, investment strategies, and a family's other financial needs. They are offered as steps to increase a student's financial aid eligibility. You must decide if they're right for you.

A date to remember: the financial aid formula starts looking at you on January 1 of the year before you apply. For the typical student, who enters college after high school graduation, that's January of the junior year. For that calendar year, the lower a family's income, the higher a student's magic number.

CHAPTER NINE

WHERE NO AID IS NEEDED

...some schools charge time, not money

Almost 20,000 students every year don't have to worry about finding money to pay for college. The cost is zero. No tuition. For most of them, no room and board.

And about 15,000 of those 20,000 are paid a salary to go to school, at one of the government's five service academies. Not bad when you figure room and board are also part of the deal.

Of course, it's extremely difficult to get in. Admission to tuition-free colleges, public or private, is among the toughest tickets in the country. Six annually accept fewer than 20 percent of the students who apply. At some, the acceptance rate is under 15 percent, lower than any Ivy League college.

And the catch: With one notable exception, students at tuition-free colleges are paying not in money but in time. The service academies require a commitment, usually five years, after graduation. At so-called "work colleges," like College of the Ozarks in Missouri and Berea in Kentucky, students hold down jobs on campus to pay their way.

The exception is the Cooper Union for the Advancement of Science and Art, on Manhattan's lower east side. It was founded by philanthropist Peter Cooper in 1859 as a haven of free education and has yet to charge its first tuition dollar.

THE SERVICE ACADEMIES

The three best-known are the U.S. Military Academy at West Point, New York, the Naval Academy at Annapolis, Maryland, and the Air Force Academy outside Colorado Springs, Colorado. Their business is training military or naval officers. Each works the same way.

Students pay on arrival a one-time fee of $1,500 for uniforms and equipment. After that, nothing. And in hardship cases, the $1,500 will be deducted from the student's $6,500-a-year salary, which he earns because he's a member of the Army, Navy, or Air Force. Graduates gain a degree and an officer's commission at the same time.

The military, naval, air force, and coast guard academies give students a free education and a modest yearly salary in exchange for a service commitment upon graduation.

The first step into one of the Big Three academies is a nomination, usually from a U.S. senator or representative. They're tough to get because each member of Congress is allowed only five nominees in each academy at any time. If your Congressman has five plebes (first-year cadets) at West Point, he won't be nominating anyone for four years. Many Congress members hold competitions among interested student-constituents to select their nominees. Nominations also are made by the president, vice president, and governors of U.S. territories.

Children of military officers can be nominated through military channels. Nominated students then must survive the same type of admission screening conducted by selective colleges, pass a physical fitness test, and meet height and weight requirements. The short and the obese are ineligible. So are married people, parents, and pregnant women. Each year, 15 percent or fewer of the students applying to each academy make it.

The U.S. Coast Guard Academy in New London, Connecticut, is identical to the Big Three in its $6,500 salary, $1,500 arrival fee, and postgraduation commitment to active duty. But it does not require a nomination. Students apply directly to the academy, like any other college. In 1993–94, the Coast Guard Academy accepted 16 percent of its applicants—the same rate as Harvard.

The U.S. Merchant Marine Academy at Kings Point, New York, trains civilians for the maritime industry. Students are members of the Naval Reserve. Like the Big Three, it requires nominations. Tuition, room, and board are free but students must pay an annual fee of about $800. Students earn no salary, just a stipend during shipboard training.

THE WORK COLLEGES

Many young people working in the country-music mecca of Branson, Missouri, wear T-shirts bearing the words "Hard Work U." They're students at College of the Ozarks, next door in Point Lookout, Missouri, where work—some of it indeed hard—replaces money.

At "work colleges" like Berea and College of the Ozarks, students work their way through school.

College of the Ozarks and Berea College in Kentucky are the best-known examples of "work colleges," designed to serve low-income students, where tuition, room, and board can be worked away. Ozarks accepts 16 percent of its applicants, Berea 32 percent.

At both schools, the FAFSA is part of the admission application. Ozarks requires 90 percent of each freshman class to have an Expected Family Contribution low enough to qualify for a Pell Grant, which goes to the college. The other 10 percent is filled by students with special talents—in sports, music, academics—and children of alumni.

Berea requires all students to show a large financial need through the FAFSA. It bases eligibility on a scale, tied to the size of the student's family, which roughly parallels the Pell formula. Berea's guidelines say a family of four needs an annual income below $34,000 to qualify; a family of nine can make it with $51,000.

Neither school charges tuition. Room, board, and fees cost $1,700 a year at Ozarks, $2,757 at Berea. Each requires students to work—15 hours a week at Ozarks, 10 to 20 hours at Berea—to cover part of the free tuition.

Freshmen get jobs such as sweeping floors, maintaining the grounds and running the power plant. Upperclassmen work in campus offices, on the student newspaper, programming computers, taking photos for brochures. Berea students staff a college-owned hotel and restaurant. Ozarks students work in the college restaurant that serves tourists overflowing from Branson.

Tour buses that come to Branson for the country music regularly visit the Ozarks campus where students conduct tours and explain the school's philosophy. Tourists are asked to leave a little something to help the cause.

Berea allows students to keep part of their hourly wages to pay room, board, and living expenses. Ozarks students get no pay but can work during the summer to earn room and board.

TYPICAL AID PACKAGE
AT TUITION-FREE SCHOOL

Here is a typical financial aid package for a student at College of the Ozarks, a tuition-free school in Point Lookout, Missouri.

Cost of Attendance	$8,750
Pell Grant	1,450
Earned by student's work	2,380
Grant from college funds	4,920
Total aid	$8,750
Cost to student	0

COOPER UNION

It's where Thomas Edison and Felix Frankfurter studied. Its Great Hall has heard both Abraham Lincoln and Bill Clinton speak. It has no tuition, no required jobs, and thus intense competition for the 210 freshman slots, especially by students attracted to life on the edge of New York's Greenwich Village.

Talented art, architecture, and engineering students can get a free college education at Cooper.

In 1993, 14 percent of Cooper's applicants were accepted. Cooper Union offers only three majors: art, architecture, and engineering. Students apply directly to one of the three schools. Art and architecture applicants must submit samples of their work. Engineering students usually have SAT math scores over 700. Unlike the work colleges, at Cooper a student's financial condition is irrelevant. The wealthy and the poor are considered equally, judged on talent. Even children of faculty get no breaks. A dean's son was rejected by Cooper, admitted at Yale.

Until a residence hall opened in 1992, Cooper students were on their own to find a place to live in the city, an expensive endeavor. Room and board in the dorm now costs $8,415 a year. All the FAFSA-triggered financial aid programs are available to help students pay living expenses in the residence hall or elsewhere.

Cooper Union also offers grants of its own money—in this case real grants, since there is no tuition to be discounted.

All tuition free-schools, public and private, are listed in most college directories.

CHAPTER TEN

THE EXPERTS SPEAK

...the questions you ask, the answers you receive

Will it cost you financial aid money if you marry your boy friend?

Does a bad credit rating hurt your chances for financial aid?

If your older brother didn't get any aid, should you bother to apply?

Do you have any hope for aid if your father makes $75,000?

Those are among more than 24,000 questions asked by USA TODAY readers since 1988 on the newspaper's annual College Admission and Financial Aid Hotline.

Every October, financial aid and admission officers from campuses across the country are invited to USA TODAY's Arlington, Virginia, headquarters. For three days, 12 hours a day, they answer calls from readers on a toll-free number appearing in the paper.

Most of the experts say they enjoy the work because it frees them from the cocoons of their offices and allows them to hear what's on the minds of folks in all parts of the country. Each expert is asked to work the phones for four hours. Some volunteer for more than one shift. In 1993, Wendy Beckemeyer of Missouri's Cottey College set the record by answering calls for 20 hours over three days.

Just about all of the questions handled in the six years of hotlines are answered in detail elsewhere in this book. But to reinforce those points, many of the questions—typical and unusual—and the answers in the experts' own words are gathered together here. The experts are named, along with the institutions at which they were connected at the time they participated in a hotline.

PERSONAL FINANCIAL SITUATION

Q. Will a bad credit rating hurt my child's chances for financial aid?

A. No. Applying for aid is not the same as applying for a bank loan. Grants and Work-Study money are not awarded on your ability to repay. And the only credit history considered for loans is the student's record with previous borrowing for college. If the student is in default, he or she is ineligible for any financial aid. — *Claire Matthews, Connecticut College.*

Q. I have two children in college. One college asks the amount of equity in our home. The other doesn't. Why?

A. Home equity is no longer considered for federal aid programs, but some colleges—usually higher-priced private schools— look at it in awarding their own aid. It's up to the college.— *Jim Lakis, Lycoming College.*

Q. I have six kids in college and I'm borrowed to the max on my home equity. But one college asks about the equity in our home. But some colleges still figure my equity into their aid formula. What can I do?

A. Explain your situation to the aid officers at those colleges. Every financial aid person can use professional judgment to depart from the rules in specific cases. With six kids in college, someone's professional judgment may give you more aid. — *Leanne Frech, University of Pittsburgh-Johnstown.*

Q. We were hurt by the Midwest floods. Will that help us get financial aid?

A. The government put more money into its programs in 1994 just for flood victims. And some financial aid officers are using professional judgment to give a break to flood victims. Be sure your college financial aid office knows about your problem. — *John Klockentager, Buena Vista College.*

Q. Must I report money in my 401-K and EE bonds on my daughter's aid form?

A. You must report your EE bonds. But the good news is that money stashed away in retirement accounts, such as a 401-K, does not have to be reported. You need only report the amount you contributed to the plan this year. — *Barry McCarty, Lafayette College.*

Q. Should I list my son's car as an asset on his financial aid form?

A. No. A car is not an asset for financial aid purposes. List only your and your son's investment assets. — *Rita Bayless, Student Aid Specialists, Inc.*

ELIGIBILITY FOR AID

Q. I'm living with my fiance. If I marry him, will it affect my chances for financial aid?

A. If you marry him, his income must be considered in deciding how much aid you get. If you stay unmarried, his income is ignored. There are reasons well beyond financial need for couples to decide whether to marry or not. But the way the system works, you are penalized for being married. If you have no spouse, there is no spouse to report. — *Barry McCarty, Lafayette College*

Q. If the financial aid formula tells me how much I'm expected to pay and the cost of my college is less than that, does that mean I should not apply for any aid?

A. Certainly not. Some aid is based on factors other than financial need. For example, any Florida resident attending a private college in Florida can get a $1,000 state grant. Other aid is available for academic talent. You won't know what you can get until you apply. — *Robin Famiglietti, Eckerd College.*

Q. I'm 41 years old. My husband and I both work. I'd like to go back to college but I'm worried about the cost. Is there any hope I could get financial aid?

A. Absolutely! Age is not a consideration in deciding eligibility. The same rules apply to you as to 18-year-olds. Apply for aid. Given the financial situation you described, you easily could be eligible. — *Wendy Beckemeyer, Cottey College.*

Q. My husband signed a pre-nuptial agreement that he won't pay college expenses for my daughter. But the college counts his income anyway and that makes her ineligible for grants. What can we do?

A. Nothing. Your husband's income pays your daughter's other bills so it must be used in determining her financial need. The pre-nuptial agreement is meaningless. — *Jamie Mowat, University of Pittsburgh-Titusville.*

Q. I'm 29 and just lost my job. Can I get aid to go to college?

A. Your chances are good. You must report last year's income on your application but attach a letter explaining you're out of work. The aid office can use professional judgment to consider current income instead of last year's. — *Robin Szitas, Allegheny College.*

Q. Our family income is $70,000 and we have home equity of $40,000. My daughter is a good student with a GPA of 3.8. Her high school counselor says she is not eligible for any money. Is that true?

A. High school counselors get very busy with other things and often don't keep up to date on financial aid. With your daughter's GPA and tough course load, I know many small private schools that would be eager to offer her financial help. Talk to a college financial aid officer. You will be pleasantly surprised.
— *Jamie Mowat, University of Pittsburgh-Titusville.*

Q. I've put money away to help my grandson pay for college. It's in a joint account in both our names. Will it hurt his eligibility for aid?

A. Yes. If your grandson's name is on the account, it will be considered as part of his resources. Change it so it's only in your name. Grandparents' assets don't have to be reported. — *Frank Valines, University of Maryland.*

Q. I'm in the military but getting out in a month. I'll be getting some veterans' benefits in a program where my contributions are matched by the government. Will that income count against me in getting financial aid?

A. It will be considered but shouldn't hurt you. And if you're a military veteran, you will be independent which usually helps.
— *Cathy McIntyre, Allentown College.*

Q. My husband makes a good income but he's going to law school next year. I have to go back to work and I'm sure we'll be making less money. Will the colleges still count my husband's salary when they calculate his financial aid?

A. They will because the form requires him to report last year's income. But he should attach an explanation of his situation and the aid office could use professional judgment to consider next year's anticipated income instead. — *Emily Delreal, Purdue University.*

Q. My income is about $100,000 a year. I have two children in college at medium-priced institutions. I was told I don't qualify for aid. Is that right?

A. Generally income that high will make you ineligible but I never tell anyone he doesn't qualify. The formula considers many other factors that could make you eligible. But you won't know unless you apply. — *Linda Renschler, Lynchburg College.*

Q. I grew up middle-class and I'm still middle-class. Why is less federal aid available to my daughter than there was for me?

A. Today's middle-class Americans have less choice in colleges, because of the higher costs, than middle-class applicants had when I got into this business in 1978. Less aid is available in the federal programs because of government spending cuts during the 1980s and because Congress has made more students eligible for aid. So a smaller amount of aid is being split into more pieces. At most schools, if you apply as late as April there's no money left regardless of your need. — *Lisa Cooper, Drury College.*

Q. Is a Canadian eligible for financial aid at U.S. colleges?

A. A noncitizen is not eligible for federal aid unless he or she has permanent resident status. But Canadians can receive colleges' own aid and often do, especially if they play hockey. — *William Mack, Rochester Institute of Technology.*

MORE THAN ONE IN COLLEGE

Q. I'm a paraplegic. My wife makes $21,000 a year. My daughter is about to go to college. I'd like to go, too. Is there any way I can afford a private school?

A. With your family income, another family member in college, and your disability, you could get full funding in financial aid at a high-cost college. — *Jamie Mowat, University of Pittsburgh-Titusville.*

Q. My son is a college freshman. My daughter is a high school senior. Will my parental contribution increase or decrease next year?

A. The parents' contribution is adjusted by the number of dependents in college carrying at least six credits. A family that does not qualify for aid with one in college may qualify with two. If your daughter's school costs twice as much as your son's, your contribution will be identical for each. Your daughter's financial need will be larger than your son's. — *Jeanne Bowen, Drew University.*

Q. I have two kids in college and am thinking of enrolling myself. Will it help their financial aid?

A. Yes. If you take at least six credits, you can divide the family contribution among three students instead of two. — *Orlo Austin, University of Illinois.*

PLANNING AHEAD FOR FINANCIAL AID

Q. I'm in ninth grade. What can I do to prepare to get financial aid for college?

A. I'll give you a four-step plan: (1) get good grades because better students often can get better aid packages; (2) develop leadership skills and other talents that colleges will find attractive; (3)

start now researching scholarships, at your school guidance office and library, that might be available to you; (4) work with your parents to save money. — *E.F. Hall, Wheeling Jesuit College.*

Q. Florida (like several other states) has a prepaid college program. I can make lump-sum payments of about $13,000 for my daughters, in seventh and third grades, to cover four years of tuition, room, and board. Is it a good idea?

A. You must decide if locking in four years of tuition at current rates is worth giving up the interest you would earn by investing that money. The average cost of college is increasing about 5 to 6 percent a year. — *Robin Famiglietti, Eckerd College.*

APPLYING FOR AID

Q. What's the best way to increase my chances for more financial aid?

A. Apply as early as possible, before the aid at your college starts to run out. And high school grades come into play when a college awards its institutional aid. Your grades are as important to financial aid as they are to being admitted. — *Barry McCarty, Lafayette College.*

Q. Do I have to be accepted at a college before I can apply for aid?

A. Absolutely not. You can apply anytime after January 1 of the year for which you request aid. And if you submit your financial information to colleges before you apply, they can give you an idea of how much aid you might get. Then you'll know if you want to follow through. — *Kathryn Dodge, Keene State College.*

Q. Must I complete my tax return before I apply for aid?

A. No. And it's best to get your application in soon after January 1 even if your taxes take longer to prepare. If you're not sure what numbers will be on your 1040, you can estimate for the aid application. — *Robin Famiglietti, Eckerd College.*

Q. If you apply to colleges in four states, must you fill out four financial aid forms?

A. No. Fill out the federal form (FAFSA) and list all four schools to receive it. If a college needs more information, it will let you know. — *Kristi Pierce, High Point College.*

Q. I'm hesitant to fill out the financial aid forms for my daughter because I worry whether the information will be confidential.

A. All the information on a financial aid form is kept confidential between you and the agency that processes it. The only authority to release it to anyone else lies with you. — *Joe Sciame, St. John's University.*

Q. Is it too late (in October) to apply for aid this year?

A. No. The deadline for applying for aid is May 1 of the academic year for which you need it. For the 1993–94 school year, you can apply until May 1, 1994. — *John Reynders, Allegheny College.*

REAPPLYING FOR AID

Q. When my oldest son started school, he didn't qualify for aid. Now a second son is going to college. Should he apply?

A. He sure should, because the chances now are better for both of your sons. The more family members in college, the less each is expected to contribute to his or her college costs. Your youngest son should apply and his brother should reapply. — *Mark Delorey, GMI Engineering and Management Institute.*

Q. If my financial situation changes after my son applies for aid, can he reapply?

A. Any student whose financial situation changes can appeal to have the aid package reconsidered. Many schools have forms for this purpose. You have nothing to lose. An appeal may not render additional aid, but at least you get their attention. — *Curtis Powell, Georgetown University.*

Q. Is it true that all colleges don't meet 100 percent of a student's financial need?

A. Unfortunately, it's true. It depends on the institution and the amount of money it has available. These days, most colleges don't have enough to meet all students' full need. — *Sheila Sauls-White, Capitol College.*

INDEPENDENT VS. DEPENDENT STUDENT

Q. My granddaughter is 20, self-supporting, and lives in a different state than her parents. But her college says she can't be "independent" for financial aid until she's 24. Why not?

A. To be independent, a student must be 24, or married, or a graduate student, or an orphan, or have a dependent other than a spouse or be a military veteran. If your granddaughter's not one of those, we have to ask why she's not living with her parents. If it's, say, due to an irrevocable family split, we can use professional judgment to declare her independent. — *William Mack, Rochester Institute of Technology.*

Q. If my kid moves out and lives on her own, is she considered independent for financial aid?

A. Not necessarily. To be independent, she must answer "yes" to one of six questions on the financial aid form. Leaving the nest isn't one of them. — *Lynell Shore, Lebanon Valley College.*

LOANS

Q. I hear that if I make six payments on my defaulted student loan, I can have my eligibility for financial aid restored. How do I do this?

A. Ask the bank you borrowed from the name of the agency managing your loan. In many cases, it will be a statewide agency such as the New York State Higher Education Services Corp. Contact that agency to set up a repayment schedule. If you make six consecutive payments on time, the agency is allowed to reinstate your eligibility. But it's not required to do so; it may insist that you pay your entire debt before it will reinstate you. — *William Mack, Rochester Institute of Technology.*

Q. I was turned down for an education loan for my son because of a bad credit rating. But your hotline experts say the bank can't look at my credit history for student loans. Who's right?

A. A student's personal credit history is not considered in the guaranteed loan program except when a student has defaulted on a previous college loan. But you're not a student. You were applying for a PLUS loan, available to parents, and banks can deny PLUS for bad credit. — *William Mack, Rochester Institute of Technology.*

Q. I'm behind on student loan payments and unemployed but I don't want to go into default. Is there anything I can do?

A. Ask the college financial aid office what agency holds your loan and apply to it for "forbearance." That will allow you to skip payments until you get a job. — *Mark Delorey, GMI Engineering and Management Institute.*

Q. I'm 47. I defaulted on a student loan many years ago. Now I'd like to go to college again, and I've made arrangements to repay the old loan but I can't get my name of the default list. So I can't get any federal aid.

A. You are ineligible for aid if you're in default. To lift your default status, find out what agency is holding your loan, contact it and convince it you are repaying. The financial aid office of your former college should know where the loan is. — *Lisa Vashon, Thomas College.*

Q. How do I get one of those low-interest loans available to every student?

A. First you must apply for need-based aid. If you get none, or if it doesn't cover the total cost of your college, you can apply to a bank for an unsubsidized student loan. Every bank must have an application form. Any student who hasn't defaulted on an earlier loan is eligible. You must pay quarterly interest but need not repay the principal until you leave school. — *Barry McCarty, Lafayette College.*

SCHOLARSHIPS

Q. What's the value of a merit scholarship in financial aid dollars?

A. It depends on the college. An institution that gets a great many applicants who are merit scholars might offer a 10 percent grant. But a school that actively recruits merit scholars would offer a full ride. If you have a merit scholarship, you already have heard from the active recruiters. — *Wendy Beckemeyer, Cottey College.*

Q. Is a scholarship search service worth the money?

A. If you want to pay someone to do something you can do for free, that's up to you. You can find the same lists of scholarships in directories and on computers at your library. If your public library doesn't have them, try a college library. — *Amber Brennan, George Washington University.*

PRIVATE VS. STATE; TWO-YEAR VS. FOUR-YEAR SCHOOLS

Q. Will my daughter get more aid at a private college than a state school?

A. Yes, if the private school costs more. Her financial need, which is her eligibility for aid, increases as the cost of her college increases. Her out-of-pocket expenses will be the same regardless of where she goes. — *Wendy Beckemeyer, Cottey College.*

Q. If I go to an out-of-state school, will it affect my chances for aid?

A. It could hurt if your state has an aid program available only to in-state students. But if the out-of-state school is more expensive, your financial need will be greater and you'll be eligible for more money. — *Joyce Farmer, Drew University.*

Q. I'm transferring from a two-year college, where I don't get financial aid, to a private four-year college. Should I reapply?

A. Definitely. At a higher-cost school, your need will be greater and you may well be eligible for aid. — *Mark Delorey, GMI Engineering and Management Institute.*

Q. My child likes an out-of-state school. I think she should stay in-state because it's less expensive. Who's right?

A. Let your child apply wherever she is interested and see what aid is offered. If an out-of-state school really likes her, it will be less expensive than you think. — *Patrick Gallivan, St. Michael's College.*

Q. I'm in the top 5 percent of my high school class and have a 29 ACT score (out of 36). I have a four-year scholarship to Iowa State but I'm applying to Harvard. What are the chances I can get a scholarship there?

A. Not good, unless your financial need is high. Iowa State wants someone with your credentials. Harvard will have a freshman class full of top students. The most selective schools like Harvard offer very little aid that isn't based on financial need. — *Tammy Cavaretta, Southern Illinois University.*

INDEX

151